The Law and Catholic Schools:

A Guide to Legal Issues for the Third Millennium

Mary Angela Shaughnessy, SCN, J.D., Ph.D.

D1096955

Second Edition, Updated & Revised

LC
501
.S53
2005

.¡12533439
#61184286

Copyright 2005
National Catholic Educational Association
1077 30th St., NW, Suite 100
Washington, D.C. 20007-3852

ISBN: 1-55833-346-0
Part No.: LEG-22-1339

TABLE OF CONTENTS

Dedication   iv

About the Author   v

Acknowledgments   vi

One   Introduction and Pre-Test   1

Two   Civil Law Affecting Catholic Education:
How Did We Get Where We Are?   31

Three   Torts: What Does the Educator Need to Know?   52

Four   Bishops, Pastors, Principals and Boards:
Rights and Responsibilities   68

Five   Parents, Students and Teachers:
Rights and Responsibilities   83

Six   Special Topics   109

Seven   A Final Reflection:
Is it Legal? Is it Ethical?
Can I Do It? Should I Do It?   152

Appendix   156

Glossary of Terms   160

Bibliography   163

DEDICATION

As a very young girl, I was the oldest of four children, the other three of whom were boys. Wonderful as they were, I wanted sisters to share our life. Finally, after eight and twelve years respectively, Janet and Karen were born into the Shaughnessy family. My sisters are wonderful family members and the best friends anyone could desire. So, this book is dedicated to them with great love and gratitude:

Janet Shaughnessy Kellogg

Karen Shaughnessy Schultz

ABOUT THE AUTHOR

Sister Mary Angela Shaughnessy, SCH, J.D., Ph.D., is a Sister of Charity of Nazareth, who has taught at all levels of Catholic education from elementary through graduate school. She served eight years as principal of a Catholic high school. Sister Mary Angela holds a bachelor's degree in English, a master's degree in English, a master's degree in educational administration, a J.D. in Law and a Ph.D. in Educational Administration and Supervision. Her research centers on the law as it affects Catholic education and Church ministry. She is the author of over twenty books.

A consultant to numerous dioceses, Sister Mary Angela is a regular speaker at the NCEA conventions. Sister has served as an adjunct professor in various college and university programs. She has served as visiting professor at the University of San Francisco since 1988. Sister has served on several White House committees through the United States Department of Education. Currently, Sister Mary Angela is Director of the Education Law Institute at Spalding University in Louisville, Kentucky. She is a member of the bar in the state of Kentucky.

Sister is the recipient of numerous awards, including the NCEA Secondary Department Award and the D'Amour/O'Neill Award for Outstanding Service to Boards of Catholic Education. In 1977, she was named one of the twenty-five most influential persons in Catholic education over the past twenty-five years. In 2005, she received the F. Sadlier Dinger Award established to honor outstanding people in the field of Catholic education.

ACKNOWLEDGMENTS

Fourteen years have passed since the publication of my text, *Catholic Schools and the Law: Approaching the New Millennium*. So much in the world, our country and our Catholic schools has changed. The legal climate around us has changed also. Issues that were not even imagined in 1991 now claim our attention. This text is an effort to update the contents of the first text and to include discussion of the many "new" issues. Many persons have walked the last thirteen years with me, and I am grateful. I express special gratitude to the many who have studied with me and who have generously shared their insights and experiences. Without them, the writing of such a text would be almost impossible.

I wish to express special gratitude to Brother Robert Bimonte, FSC, Executive Director of the Department of Elementary Schools of the National Catholic Educational Association, who is a true friend and colleague in the great ministry that is Catholic education.

I also wish to acknowledge the support of the administration of Spalding University (Louisville, KY), who have given me the time and resources to devote to the study of Catholic education law. I particularly wish to thank my assistant, Joan Danner, who keeps me organized and able to move from one task to the next.

I thank my family, especially the next generation, whose years in Catholic schools continue to provide me with inspiration for my writing. I thank my religious community, the Sisters of Charity of Nazareth, who support my ministry.

Finally, I thank you, the reader. I hope that this text will offer you support and insight in your ministry.

Mary Angela Shaughnessy, SCN

January, 2005

CHAPTER ONE

INTRODUCTION and PRE-TEST

Fourteen years have passed since the appearance of the text, *The Law and Catholic Schools: Approaching the New Millennium*, which was written as an attempt to gather as much legal information concerning Catholic education as possible into one volume. So many aspects of Catholic education have changed over the years. The numbers of religious and priests in Catholic schools have continued to decline, while the laity continue to provide strong, effective leadership and it is they who will largely set the future of Catholic education. Unfortunately, many Catholic schools have closed due to changing demographics and the rising costs of providing Catholic education. Certainly, the values that drive Catholic education remain very strong. However, the legal situation has undergone dramatic changes. Fourteen years ago, very few people could have predicted the sexual abuse crisis in the Catholic Church, a crisis that has saddened the faithful, and made many, including Catholic educators, extremely fearful.

This text will include topics either not discussed or only barely mentioned in the pre-cursor text including: confidentiality, boundaries, harassment and bullying, the Internet, e-mail, health issues, violence, special needs, and copyright law. Certainly, the horizon of legal issues in Catholic schools has widened beyond anything most educators would have imagined in 1991.

This text will first offer a pre-test that will allow readers to assess their degree of legal knowledge. After one has taken the test, one can "correct" it and read the explanations for the answers.

Chapter II offers an overview of civil law as it affects Catholic education. In order to understand that law, it is necessary to spend some time considering the law that impacts public education. The reader may be surprised to learn that, despite some real differences, there are many similarities.

Chapter III will discuss tort law, particularly the law of negligence, which is the most often litigated tort. Chances are, if a principal or educator is sued for any action or inaction, the allegation will be one of negligence. Although recent times have seen newspaper and other media reports offering detailed reports on the sexual abuse crisis, negligence remains the more common threat.

Chapter IV will discuss the rights and responsibilities of bishops, pastors, principals and boards, as i.e. the types of Catholic schools found in the United States and the types of boards governing, or advising those who administer, Catholic schools. Chapter V will offer some insights into the rights and responsibilities of parents, students and teachers.

Chapter VI will discuss selected legal issues presented by the topics cited above which were not discussed in the earlier text. Finally, Chapter VII will offer a closing reflection and some recommendations for "lawful" ministry in Catholic education.

So, the author invites you to take the 20-question pre-test.

Legal Pre-test:
How Much Do You Already Know?

Please answer True or False.

_____ 1. Teachers and students in Catholic schools have the same Constitutional protections as those in the public sector.

_____ 2. It is never legally permissible to leave students under the age of 18 unattended.

_____ 3. Persons should be told what it is they have done "wrong" and allowed to present their side(s) of the story before penalties are imposed.

_____ 4. If a principal grants due process in disciplinary proceedings, the teacher or student must also be allowed to bring legal counsel to any internal proceedings.

_____ 5. If a teacher believes that a student is a troublemaker, that belief should be noted in writing.

_____ 6. The Supreme Court has ruled that desks and lockers can only be searched if a proper search warrant is obtained.

_____ 7. An at will employee can be terminated for any reason.

_____ 8. If parents have signed a field trip release form, the school cannot be held liable for any injuries that do occur.

_____ 9. Americans with Disabilities Act requires that employers hire persons with disabilities and provide any needed accommodation.

_____ 10. Teachers can be required to retire at age 75.

_____ 11. Catholic schools can discriminate against students with special needs.

_____ 12. A principal can be held liable for the actions or inactions of employees.

_____ 13. Every person who volunteers in a school must be screened.

_____ 14. If a principal fails to give employees instructions re: child abuse reporting laws, the school could be held liable for damages.

_____ 15. Emotional abuse, like physical abuse, is forbidden by law.

_____ 16. Catholic school employees can be disciplined for off-campus behavior.

_____ 17. Teachers and administrators should respect the confidences entrusted to them and never reveal them.

_____ 18. A school and its administrators can be held liable for harassment, including sexual harassment.

_____ 19. In the absence of a court order, a non-custodial parent has no right to obtain information about his or her child.

_____ 20. What one may legally do may not be the most moral or ethical action to take.

Answers and Discussion

1. Teachers and students in Catholic schools have the same Constitutional protections as those in the public sector. **FALSE.**

Most persons taking this test, or attending a school law lecture or workshop for the first time, believe that this statement is "true." Indeed, it sounds as if it should be true. After all, in the United States isn't everyone guaranteed Constitutional protections? The answer is that the United States government guarantees that it and its agents will protect the Constitutional rights of all persons in their institutions and programs. The Constitution is completely silent as to what private institutions and their agents may do, and leaves any such regulation of private activity to the state and its legislatures. For example, the First Amendment to the United States Constitution states: *"Congress shall make no law respecting an establishment of religion...."* This directive ensures that there will be no state religion and that persons will not be forced to abandon their personal religious beliefs in favor of those that the state or its agents might wish them to accept.

Public schools are state agencies and those who staff them must recognize and respect the Constitutional rights of those who work and study in them. As a private entity, a Catholic school or program has no such stricture. Catholic schools may have rules and regulations that the public school may not have. For example, in a Catholic school, teachers can be forbidden to express opinions contrary to the teachings of the Catholic Church. A Catholic schoolteacher could be prohibited from taking a public pro-choice stance and from telling students that, for example: *"responsible persons limit the size of their families and take the pill."* A public school could not impose such restrictions on its employees because the First Amendment also guarantees free speech to those in its institutions.

Some Catholic school personnel are aghast to learn that they do not have freedom of expression while in the Catholic school. Yet, why else does a Catholic school exist if not to further the mission of the Catholic Church? It is true that Catholic schools strive to operate excellent educational programs. In fact, canon law requires that the education in Catholic schools be at least as outstanding as that offered in public schools. This author has often stated that the first legal obligation of a Catholic school, after, of course, ensuring the safety of everyone within their walls, is to be true to the teachings of the Catholic Church. If a school presents itself as Catholic, it is subject to the bishop of the diocese in which it is located and can and should be required to adhere to the magisterium or teaching authority of the Catholic Church.

Some parents, particularly ones who are not Catholic, as well as some who are Catholic, may choose a Catholic school for reasons other than religious ones. They may respect the academic program of the school, such as the wide range of extra-curricular activities available, or seek certain athletic opportunities for their children. Nonetheless, a Catholic school must be both "Catholic" and a "school."

2. It is never legally permissible to leave students under the age of 18 unattended.
   FALSE.

Most readers of this text will recall a principal or other supervisor firmly advising teachers that students are *"never to be left unattended."* Indeed, such was the prevailing wisdom. If, however, one were to ask a group of assembled teachers how many of them could honestly say that they had never left students unattended, few, if any, teachers would answer in the affirmative. Obviously, no one wants to encourage teachers to leave students unattended cavalierly. However there are circumstances in which the prudent action to take is, indeed, to leave students unattended. If a teacher needs to use the restroom, for example, he or she may leave students unattended for a reasonable amount of time. In the case of an emergency, for which courts have not provided a definition, students can be left unattended.

Should a student be injured while the teacher was out of the room or area, the court would apply the "reasonable teacher" test. Did the teacher act the way one would expect a reasonably prudent teacher to act? If a teacher learns that an emergency exists in the hallway and no other staff member can be summoned, the reasonable teacher would leave the classroom and its students unattended and go into the hallway to deal with the emergency. If a student in the classroom is injured in the absence of the teacher, the teacher may, as indicated above, avoid liability if the judge and/or jury finds his or her actions to be reasonable, in light of all the circumstances.

Courts do expect that teachers will have told students what the expectations are if the teacher has to leave the room. At a minimum, students should be instructed to remain in their seats and work quietly. Many elementary classrooms display posted rules and one rule might be: *"If no adult is in the room, students will remain seated."* Of course, one has to give age appropriate directions.

Additionally, courts expect that teachers will take the age of their students into consideration when absenting themselves from their classrooms or areas. The principle: *"the younger the child chronologically or mentally, the greater the standard of care,"* will generally govern the situation. Therefore, more latitude can be afforded the actions of a teacher of eighth graders or high school students than those of pre-school or kindergarten students. Chapter III will discuss in detail the concept of negligence, which governs cases alleging student injury.

3. Persons should be told what it is they have done "wrong" and allowed to present their side(s) of the story before penalties are imposed.
   TRUE.

Reasonable teachers who are striving to be fair in their dealings with students will want to take the time to listen to a student's version of a story before disciplining the student. The reality, however, may well be that the harried teacher who has just watched the student commit an infraction does not see any need for listening to a "story." Yet, things are not always what they seem. Maybe John did punch Joe, but did Joe do something to provoke John? Provocation will not excuse John, but it might mitigate the punishment. Perhaps everyone reading this text has had the experience of being absolutely convinced that a student did something that was wrong, only to discover later that the conviction was a mistaken one. Perhaps closer to home, most readers will recall times when teachers accused them of misdeeds they did not do and the teachers would not listen. Every educator who wishes to be fair will take the time, even it seems a "waste of time" to listen to an accused student's story.

In the public sector, this listening to someone's side of a story is called procedural due process, which will be discussed in detail in Chapter 2. While the Catholic school educator is not bound by all the requirements of Constitutional procedural due process, the teacher is expected to be "fair" and to follow the first three elements of procedural due process, which constitute the requirements for "good faith and fair dealing," which do bind everyone: (1) notice and (2) a hearing (3) before an impartial tribunal.

4. If a principal grants due process in disciplinary proceed-
    ings, the teacher or student must also be allowed to bring
    legal counsel to any internal proceedings.
    FALSE.

The right to bring counsel is a Constitutional one, guaranteed by the Fifth and Fourteenth Amendments to the United
States Constitution. It is one of the procedural due process
rights guaranteed to those who deal with government agencies.
It is not required of individuals in private institutions and
programs.

There is a common sense reason, as well as a legal one, for
not permitting legal counsel to attend internal proceedings. If
the accused student or teacher is allowed to bring an attorney
to a hearing, then the school will have to be represented by an
attorney who attends the proceedings. Attorneys play two
roles. They are both advocates for their clients and adversaries
of those who oppose their clients. If two attorneys are present
during disciplinary hearings, the situation may quickly
become adversarial and any hope of reconciliation may disap-
pear. This author once heard a superintendent observe:
*"Attorneys belong in courtrooms where the judges can keep
them in line. They do not belong in schools."* There is truth in
that statement. Catholic schools are not courtrooms and
administrators have a right to determine who will be present at
such hearings. Parents should always be allowed to attend
suspension and expulsion hearings, if they so desire.
Employees facing disciplinary action should be able to bring a
witness, if desired.

While Catholic education, like all programs and institutions in this country, is subject to the legal process, administrators should be aware of what is required. Permitting lawyers
to attend disciplinary hearings in the school is not required.

5. If a teacher believes that a student is a troublemaker, that belief should be noted in writing.
FALSE.

The law of defamation of character governs this statement. Teachers must be very careful about what they write concerning the behavior and motivation of students. Whatever is written should follow three rules: (1) it should be specific; (2) it should be behaviorally-oriented; and, (3) it should be verifiable. "Troublemaker" is not a specific term. What one person may deem behavior making a student a "troublemaker," another person may find creative or innovative.

Most readers will recall a parent or other significant adult advising them in words similar to: *"Don't put anything in black and white that you wouldn't want to read on the front page of the newspaper."* This advice is as valid today as it was decades ago. Before committing any statements to writing, the educator should ask: *"Is it necessary or important that I write this?"* If the answer is *"yes,"* then: *"How can I write this in a way that is specific, behaviorally oriented and verifiable?"*

Chapter III will discuss defamation of character in greater detail. For the purposes of this chapter, the reader should note that while libel, i.e., written defamation, is easier to prove, spoken defamation or slander poses dangers as well.

6. The Supreme Court has ruled that desks and lockers can only be searched if a proper search warrant is obtained.
FALSE.

The United States Supreme Court, in the 1985 case, *New Jersey v. T.L.O.*, ruled that public school personnel do not have to procure a search warrant prior to conducting a search of students. In this case, a teacher brought a female student to the vice-principal and accused her of smoking, an accusation she denied. The vice-principal opened her purse and found marijuana, rolling papers, an account book, and a substantial amount of money. He turned the evidence over to the police who charged the girl with criminal offenses of which she was later found guilty and adjudicated a juvenile delinquent.

T.L.O., the female student, alleged that the search was improper because it was conducted without a search warrant. If the search was improper, the fruit of the search must be excluded from criminal proceedings under a doctrine known as "the fruit of the poisonous tree," i.e. if the tree, the search, is poisoned, then the fruit, the evidence that is found, is poisoned as well and cannot be utilized against the defendant. The United States Supreme Court disagreed and held that public schools were not bound by the same constraints that bind law enforcement officials. The court ruled that students in schools do not and should not have the same "reasonable expectations of privacy" as do adults. Thus, so long as a school official has a reason, which in T.L.O.'s case would be the teacher's accusation, a search may be conducted and the fruit of the search used in criminal proceedings. This topic will be explored further in Chapter III.

7. An at-will employee can be terminated for any reason.
    FALSE.

The doctrine of at-will employment is based on old English common law governing the relationship of master and servant, the concept of which will be discussed in Chapter II. This doctrine allowed the employer, the master, to hire and fire whomever he wished for any reason he wished. It was often stated that an employer could fire a person for no reason, a good reason, or a bad reason. This doctrine governed private employment for many years. By 1960, courts at least beginning to consider the possibility that the right to fire someone for a "bad" reason without any consequences was not absolute. The first case in which the employee "won" was the 1959 *Peterman v. International Brotherhood of Teamsters Local 396*, which held that an employer could be held liable for firing someone who refused to commit perjury to keep his job. This case and later cases began the development of what is now called "wrongful discharge." While no court to date has required a Catholic school to keep in its employ an employee that administrators have dismissed, courts have held that even private employers may have to pay damages to employees who are dismissed for "bad" reasons, generally reasons that violate public policy, such as refusing to perform illegal acts.

Certainly, Catholic school administrators will want to avoid terminations that violate public policy. At the same time, however, administrators need to understand that non-renewal of contract is not synonymous with termination. A contract is for a determined, specific amount of time. Theoretically, no one is under any obligation to renew the contract, unless there is some agreed-upon stipulation in the contract which automatically renews the contract. Administrators must be very careful to use the proper phraseology when informing persons that their employment will not continue into the next year. One should say: *"I am not renewing your contract next year,"* or *"Your contract will not be renewed,"* rather than, *"I am letting you go,"* or *"I am terminating you,"* or *"I am firing you."* Hiring and firing issues will be discussed in greater detail later in the text.

8. If parents have signed a field trip release form, the school cannot be held liable for any injuries that do occur.
    FALSE.

The correct response to this statement is "false" because parents and guardians cannot "sign away" their children's right to safety or absolve educators of the responsibility to take reasonable care of their children.

Educators have been discussing field trips for years and it may appear that little could be left to say on the subject. However, this writer continues to get many queries concerning field trips, so some discussion of this topic is in order. Since this is one of the most frequently requested topics addressed in school law seminars and workshops, it is appropriate to give some general guidelines here. A more general discussion of the topic of negligence will be given in Chapter III. Field trips have long been part of the educational experience in schools. ministry. Educators want young people to see that learning is not confined to the school building. Field trips give children and adolescents the opportunity to apply knowledge learned in classroom or other educational settings to "real life" situations. At the same time, most educators are aware that field trips pose special legal issues.

More accidents involving young persons occur in classrooms or other school meeting places than in all other activities, because such places are where students spend much of their time. However, off-campus activities are more dangerous than classroom activities simply because of their nature and the hazards involved in transportation. Some attorneys have adopted a "no field trip" position on the theory that if young people are not taken off site, they cannot get hurt off campus. Most educators, however, view field trips as an important part of a young person's education and formation. The challenge is to balance the risks and the benefits of field trips effectively.

Educational Purpose

Most attorneys and judges would probably agree that a field trip should have an educational or programmatic purpose. If an accident were to occur, school administrators could much more easily justify an educational trip than one that is purely recreational in nature.

A Michigan case, *Davis v. Homestead Farms*, illustrates this. A horse bit a kindergarten student while she was participating in a field trip to a farm. The court found that the trip to the farm constituted a curricular activity and suggested a balancing test of risks and benefits. Taking kindergarten children to a farm is definitely educational. While there is some risk involved, parents had to have accepted the risk when they accepted the benefit. In the absence of any evidence indicating that the school failed to provide adequate supervision, the school was held blameless.

Educational purposes should be readily apparent. Eighth grade "rites of passage" type of trips to amusement parks generally do not fall into the category of educational trips. In an effort to attract such trips, many amusement parks now distribute information suggesting how such trips can be made educational.

Lesson plans, such as *"Teaching Physics from the Ferris Wheel,"* may be offered. An argument can certainly be made that a trip to an amusement park can be educational. However, the administrator must ensure that there is adequate preparation for the academic or programmatic aspect of the trip and that the teacher or supervisor can use the experience as a basis for further discussion.

A cover letter, stating the educational purpose of the trip might accompany each permission slip. Virtually every diocese has a standard permission form included in its policies and procedures. All school and program administrators should use this form and this form only.

In the unfortunate case in which a student is injured, a school and its administrators will be in a much better legal position if the educational value of the field trip is clearly evident. Administrators will find it very difficult to justify a trip that was taken purely for pleasure.

Liability for Injury

As stated above, parents cannot sign away their children's rights to safety. Parishes, schools, and their employees and volunteers are required to protect the safety of the children entrusted to their care. If a child is injured while participating in a field trip and evidence indicates that the supervising adults failed in their duty to supervise adequately and if that failure was a significant factor in the student's sustaining an injury, the school and/or its employees can be held liable for injury.

Some people ask: *"Why have a permission form if you can be held liable anyway?"* While the permission form does not provide absolute protection from all liability for injury, it does provide the best protection available. If an unforeseeable event occurred, such as a child hit by a drunk driver or injured when a tool falls from a scaffold, there is a very strong possibility that the school and its employees will be exonerated from blame, since no school official or agent violated a duty or took an action that caused, or contributed to, the injury.

The mythical creature, "the reasonable person," is the standard courts use when considering liability. A court will ask: *"Did the adult supervise the young person in a manner that a reasonable person in the same situation could be expected to do? Did a parent sign the permission form? What exactly did the form say?"* The answers to these questions will determine the nature and degree of liability.

Permission Forms

Diocesan or, in the case of schools not owned by the diocese, other attorney-approved forms should be used. If the trip poses special risks, e.g., proximity to bodies of water, these should be noted either in the cover letter, or in an addendum to the form. Indicating the educational or programmatic purpose of the trip is also advisable.

Submitted permission slips should be checked for forgery. The person responsible for the trip could be required to check signatures with those on file on a signature card. Perhaps the school secretary could be given the task of checking all field trip signatures. When one person consistently checks all forms, the likelihood of finding forgeries increases.

A young person who does not have a signed permission form should not be allowed to participate in the outing. A non-standard form such as a handwritten note saying: *"Bobby can go with you today,"* should not be accepted, as a parent could always maintain that he or she was not aware of the real destination, educational, or programmatic purpose or risks involved in the trip. If the school administrator wishes to fax the form to a parent who will sign and return it, that is permissible.

Transportation

The means of transportation should be clearly noted in the cover letter or the permission slip, unless only one mode of transportation is ever used and that fact is noted in the parent/student handbook. As far as possible, buses should be used for field trips. If parent drivers are used, the permission slip should contain a clause in which the parent agrees to this mode of transportation. If the parish or school does not have insurance covering volunteer drivers, parent drivers should be so notified. Since even those policies offering some coverage to parent and other volunteer drivers generally only apply after all the driver's insurance has been exhausted, drivers should be required to place a copy of their proof of auto insurance on file, and should be told that they can be held liable in the event of accident or injury. The same cautions apply when teachers drive their own cars to transport students. Thus the use of teacher cars should be discouraged. Administrators should consult their insurance agents or the appropriate archdiocesan officials in this matter.

Overnight Trips

Both elementary and high school age students may participate in overnight trips, such as retreats or field trips to places of historical significance, such as Washington, D.C. The standard permission form should be used. Chaperons should have notarized medical releases for the young persons, which allow the procurement of medical attention for injured or ill participants.

The permission form should clearly state the penalties to be imposed if rules are broken. For example, violations of civil law and use of alcohol or drugs probably should result in a student's being sent home. The permission form might include a statement such as: *"We/I agree to arrange transportation home for (name of child) in the event of serious infractions of a rule or rules."*

At the high school level, trips to foreign countries are also a concern; such trips are beginning to involve elementary students as well. Administrators should ensure that only reputable companies are retained for such trips and can provide proof of insurance. An administrator must understand that if the parish or school advertises the trip and supplies the adult supervisors who chaperon the trip, the parish or school cannot evade its responsibility for the trip; in effect, the trip is a parish or school-sponsored trip. At the time of the writing of this text, many questions still remain in terms of air travel safety as well as passenger screening. If administrators decide that a trip involving air travel is going to be offered, the permission slip should have parents clearly acknowledge that they accept the possibility that serious injury and death can occur.

Administrators frequently ask about the possibility of parents being entirely responsible for trips and the school having no responsibility for what happens on those trips. If the administrator allows fundraising in the program or school, dissemination of materials, etc., a court could well find that the trip is school or program-sponsored.

Finally, the decision to take a field trip is one that should not be made lightly. The wise administrator weighs the risks and benefits posed by the trip in making a final determination.

9. The Americans with Disabilities Act requires that employers hire persons with disabilities and provide any needed accommodation.
FALSE.

No law, federal or state, requires that employers hire persons with disabilities and provide any accommodation that the prospective employee might need. Rather, the law requires that employers not discriminate against otherwise qualified applicants on the basis of disability if, with reasonable accommodation, the applicant can perform the essential functions of the job. There is still some discussion as to whether the ADA applies to schools operated by religious groups. However, most state law now requires that persons with disabilities be treated fairly in all job considerations. Regardless of whether the law requires it, a Catholic school administrator will want to be fair. All persons should be evaluated fairly on the basis of their abilities and fitness for the position.

If, for example, a legally-blind person were to seek a position teaching English in a Catholic school and the only accommodation needed was the ability to magnify materials, school administrators should not eliminate the individual from consideration solely because he is legally blind. The school is not required to give preference to the individual because he is disabled, however. Therefore, if after a careful, objective consideration of all applicants and their qualifications, school officials decide to offer the job to an applicant who is not disabled, it does not necessarily follow that the school discriminated against the person with the disability. Should such an applicant file a lawsuit claiming discrimination, school officials would probably be required to articulate a non-discriminatory reason for the selection: the successful applicant had more experience, more degrees, etc. Some courts have even upheld reasons such as: *"the applicant we selected will fit in better with the people who are already here."*

The key point in this discussion is that civil law requires all employers to be fair in their dealings with employees and potential employees. The Gospel, of course, demands such fairness from all who profess to follow a Christian way of life.

10. Teachers can be required to retire at age 75.
    FALSE.

Most readers will be able to remember the days when mandatory retirement occurred at age 65 or, if there were no mandatory retirement age, 65 was generally the age at which one could retire. Various theories abound as to why the age of 65 was selected. One theory holds that this age was picked when Social Security was established, as most persons did not live to the age of 65. Another theory bases the age on an old Roman practice of pensioning off soldiers at that age on the theory that if they had lived that long, they were entitled to government support. Regardless of the theory, today there is no age at which retirement can be required. No one can be denied employment simply on the basis of advanced years.

As baby boomers continue to age, one can expect that more and more "older" persons will be in the job market. Administrators must focus clearly on job related issues – does the individual possess the necessary physical and mental qualifications to be hired for, or to continue in, the job? Discussions of age must be avoided.

11. Catholic schools can discriminate against students with special needs.
    FALSE.

As the above discussions on disability in employment demonstrate, no one is allowed to discriminate on the basis of disability. However, Catholic and other private school officials are not required to accept students with special needs. What Catholic school administrators need to keep in mind is really two-fold: what civil law requires and what the Gospel demands.

Civil law requires that all persons be treated and evaluated fairly. The Gospel demands no less. Jesus said: *"Let all the little children come to me."* He did not say: *"Let all the little normal children come to me."* While there are some happy exceptions, historically Catholic schools have not done a good job of meeting the needs of special children. Far too many Catholic schools have adopted a policy statement such as: *"This school is not able to provide services for students with learning disabilities. Therefore, students with special needs should not apply and will not be considered for admission."* Such a statement is illegal and not in accordance with the Gospel or Church teaching. Everyone in the Catholic Church has a right to access the services of the Church. Education is one such service.

The above is not meant to suggest that Catholic schools must admit every student with special needs and provide programs of study to address them. Catholic school administrators need to ensure that students with special needs seeking admission to their schools are evaluated as fairly as all other students. As will be discussed in Chapter VI, financial exigency is always a reason to decline to admit a student. For example, if a student needs a full-time aide, the school will not ordinarily be expected to provide one and so the school can decline admission. If the parents are willing to underwrite the cost of the aide, the school should be willing to consider admission.

Inability to meet the needs of students is not the same thing as inconvenience in meeting the needs of students. It may not be convenient for the teacher or the school to allow a student to take untimed tests or to have an aide administer tests orally, but it is not impossible.

While being careful to try to meet the needs of students who can be successful with reasonable accommodations, school officials must be careful not to admit students whose needs the school cannot meet. Once admitted, a student has a far greater claim on time and resources than does one who is merely seeking admission. Administrators need to examine policies and procedures carefully to ensure both fairness and feasibility of delivering services.

12. A principal can be held liable for the actions or inactions of employees.
TRUE.

The legal doctrine of *respondeat superior:* let the superior answer, can hold superiors responsible for the actions of subordinates. If a teacher is absent from her classroom when a student is injured and a court deems the absence unreasonable, the principal can be held liable if it can be shown that the principal knew teachers routinely left students unattended and took no action to correct the situation. Principals, then, must ensure that teachers know what the school's expectations for teacher behaviors and that teachers are well-versed in policies and procedures.

13. Every person who volunteers in a school must be screened.
FALSE.

At the time of the writing of this text (2005), the statement is false. Every state does not require that every volunteer in a school be screened. The statement would be "true" if the word "should" were substituted for the word "must" as in "Every person who volunteers in a school should be screened."

In light of the Bishops' Charter, many dioceses are now mandating that persons who volunteer more than a single time in a school be fingerprinted or otherwise screened. However, there are still situations in which screening has not been mandated. For example, if a mother comes to school, collects bookkeeping work and takes it home to complete, some school administrators would not screen the parent. However, a parent who routinely volunteers as an aide in a fourth grade classroom would be screened.

Realizing that some readers may find this suggestion extreme, this author suggests that the day is not too far off when every parent who enrolls his or her child in a school will be screened. Catholic schools can set such requirements. While some parents may find such a practice objectionable, they should understand that the reason for it is the protection of children-theirs and all students enrolled in the school. Parents should be informed that conviction of a crime is not an automatic bar to volunteering. A general rule of thumb is ten years; if a parent stole a car twenty years ago and was convicted, but has lived an exemplary life since, the theft conviction should probably not keep the parent from volunteering. Obviously, some offenses are treated differently. A person with a conviction for child abuse should never be allowed to volunteer or have unsupervised contact with students. The risk is simply too great.

14. If a principal fails to give employees instructions re: child abuse reporting laws, the school could be held liable for damages.
   TRUE.

Under the doctrine of *respondeat superior* discussed above, the principal or other superior can be held liable for the actions or omissions of those they supervise. Therefore, if a teacher violates state child abuse reporting laws by failing to report suspected child abuse and if it can be shown that the principal never made the laws available to employees, never referenced them in meetings, and had no policies and procedures regarding the reporting of abuse, the principal could be held liable.

One of the most serious issues confronting those involved in the ministry of Catholic education today is child abuse.

Teachers and other employees are in a particularly sensitive position. Students often choose teachers as confidants in their struggles to deal with abuse and its effects. For this reason, boards of education and principals must ensure that teachers and all other school employees are as prepared as possible to deal with the realities of abuse and neglect. Administrators should consider adopting a policy such as: *"This school or program abides by the child abuse reporting statutes of the state."* Further, policy should require that principals and other administrators spend some time reviewing pertinent state law and school policies and providing information and discussion on the topic at one of the first faculty meetings of the year. If a separate meeting is not provided for other employees and volunteers, such as secretaries, custodians, and cafeteria workers, the administrator should consider having them present for the appropriate portion of the faculty or staff meeting.

Statutory considerations

All fifty states have laws requiring educators to report suspected abuse and/or neglect. While the actual wording varies from state to state, the statute will ordinarily require that persons who supervise children or adolescents report suspected child abuse. Some states are now requiring anyone with knowledge of possible abuse to report it. Compliance with these statutes may not be as easy as it first appears. What arouses suspicion in one adult may not in another. Some statutes mention "reasonable suspicion." These standards could result in two teachers' viewing the same situation and reaching two completely different conclusions. In such cases, courts have to determine whether each individual sincerely believed in the correctness of his or her perception. Despite the best of intentions and efforts, teachers and other staff members may fail to report suspected child abuse. If, however, the administrator can demonstrate that the board has an appropriate policy in place and the administrator has appropriately implemented it, responsibility for failure to report should be that of the individual who failed, not of the institution.

Statutes generally mandate reporting procedures. The reporting individual usually makes a phone report that is followed by a written report within a specified time period, often 48 hours, although some states do have different procedures.

Statutes usually provide protection for a person who makes a good-faith report of child abuse that later is discovered to be unfounded. Such a good-faith reporter will not be liable to the alleged abuser for defamation of character. However, a person can be held liable for making what is referred to as a "malicious report," one which has no basis in fact and which was made by a person who knows that no factual basis existed. Conversely, statutes usually mandate that a person who knew of child abuse or neglect and failed to report it can be fined and/or charged with a misdemeanor or felony.

15. Emotional abuse, like physical abuse, is forbidden by law. **TRUE**.

Only a few years ago, emotional abuse was rarely, if ever, discussed. Social service agencies and police departments had their proverbial hands full dealing with sexual and physical abuse. Today, instances of emotional, psychological, and mental abuse, as well as physical and sexual abuse, are being investigated. It is no longer rare for a teacher to be accused of emotional abuse. Before one can adequately distinguish among the types of abuse, a discussion of what constitutes abuse may be in order.

Defining Abuse

What is child abuse? This author once heard an attorney define it as *"corporal punishment gone too far."* Although it excludes sexual and emotional abuse, the definition has merit. However, it poses questions: How far is too far? Who makes the final determination? Can what one person considers abuse be considered valid parental corporal punishment by another? Are there any allowances for differing cultural practices? It is difficult, if not impossible, to give a precise definition that will cover all eventualities. Certainly, some situations are so extreme that there can be little argument that physical abuse has occurred. Someone has abused a student who appears at school with cigarette burns. When a child alleges sexual abuse, the investigating agency will have to determine whether the child is telling the truth, lying, or somehow mistaken. The investigating agency will have to determine which conclusion is the true one.

Emotional abuse is much harder to substantiate. Due to the sheer overload of cases in which physical injuries are alleged, emotional abuse cases must be fairly extreme before investigators will respond. Raising one's voice is not emotional abuse; telling a student he or she is "stupid" might well be.

The majority of cases will probably not be clear-cut, and an educator may well struggle to decide if a report should be made. Many law enforcement officials and some attorneys instruct educators to report everything that students tell them that could possibly constitute abuse or negligence. They further caution teachers and other adults that it is not their job to determine if abuse has occurred. As a mandated reporter, the teacher has a responsibility to present the information to the agency designated to receive reports. Appropriate officials will determine whether the report should be investigated further or simply "screened out" as a well-intentioned report that does not appear to be in the category of abuse.

In-service Education

Administrators should provide professional staff, other employees, and volunteers with some in-service training concerning the indicators of child abuse and neglect and the legal procedures for reporting such conditions. There are many excellent written resources available. Local police departments and social service agencies are usually happy to make both materials and speakers available to schools and programs. If an institution does not provide its staff members with education and materials on this topic, a phone call to appropriate sources should provide the needed materials.

16. Catholic school employees can be disciplined for off-campus behavior.
TRUE.

Some persons taking this test or similar instruments may be surprised to learn that this statement is true. While persons readily concede that school policies and procedures govern their behavior while they are working, they find it hard to believe that those same policies and procedures, as well as others, can govern their "off duty" behavior. A Catholic schoolteacher or other employee is a role model and, as such, has certain responsibilities. If a Catholic school teacher is arrested for driving under the influence of alcohol, it is highly likely that the newspaper report will mention the individual's employment as a Catholic school teacher while, in similar circumstances, another person's place of employment is not mentioned.

Principals are often confronted with issues of actual or perceived inappropriate staff conduct and may wonder what legal rights they have to demand certain standards of behavior from staff members, particularly during off-campus times. What a staff member does, both in and outside the educational setting, impacts the quality and integrity of ministry within the setting. The doctrine of separation of church and state protects Catholic schools and their administrators and allows them to set standards of personal behavior that would not be permitted in the public sector.

Behavioral Expectations for Catholic Educators

Documents governing employment should state that staff members are expected to support the teachings of the

Catholic Church through their behavior. More than a few schools have non-Catholic staff members and one would not expect such individuals to attend Mass outside the school on a regular basis or to be participating members of a parish. But non-Catholics who seek to acquire or retain positions in Catholic settings should expect that standards of behavior would be in force. For example, if the fact that an individual had an abortion becomes known and is a source of scandal, then school administrators have every right to terminate that individual's employment or volunteer status. To do otherwise might send a confusing message to parents, students, and the larger community.

Issues of Sexual Preference and/or Lifestyle

While a broader discussion of staff behavior will be undertaken in Chapter VI, issues of sexual preference and lifestyle, which can pose special problems, should be mentioned here. While no one should condemn a homosexual orientation, a Catholic educational administrator as an agent of the Church cannot ignore manifestations of a gay lifestyle that pose scandal.

Equally difficult decisions must be made in situations involving divorced staff members who remarry without an annulment if that fact becomes known. There is no easy solution, but administrators and others with policy responsibilities for Catholic schools have an obligation to see that the teachings of the Catholic Church are respected and not compromised in the witness given by staff members. Many diocesan policies are concerned with scandalous public behavior; board members and administrators should use diocesan policies as a basis for parish and school policies.

In summary, then, once an individual performs an act that is inconsistent with Church teaching and that act becomes publicly known, that person may no longer be qualified to minister in a given situation at that time. While such a reality may seem obvious, it is recommended that documents state the requirement of supporting the teachings of the Church.

17. Teachers and administrators should respect the confidences entrusted to them and should never reveal them. **FALSE.**

Most readers will have heard at least one story involving a teacher who received a student confidence, failed to act on the knowledge, and the student later harmed self or others. Some teachers mistakenly believe that they are protected by a privilege, which allows them to keep information shared by students confidential. There really are only two privileges that are still recognized by courts in this country: priest/penitent and attorney/client. If a student tells a teacher that he is thinking about killing himself and the teacher does not tell a parent or school supervisor and the student later kills himself, recent case law indicates that the teacher can be charged with negligent homicide and voluntary or involuntary manslaughter, all of which are crimes.

While the topic of confidentiality will be discussed later in the text, readers should be aware at the onset that students should be told in age-appropriate language: *"I will keep your confidence so long as no one's life, health, or safety is involved. Once they are involved, there is no confidentiality."*

18. A school and its administrators can be held liable for harassment, including sexual harassment. **TRUE.**

A school and its administrators, as well as teachers, can be held liable for harassment if they knew about it and took no action or if they should have known about it. They will not be held liable for harassment of which they had no knowledge and for which there was no reasonable expectation that they should have known about it.

There is, of course, harassment that consists of behavior that is annoying or demeaning, but is not sexual. Bullying is a type of harassment. The growing practice of hazing is also a type of harassment. Sexual harassment is becoming more commonplace and demands a zero tolerance policy. This topic will also be discussed in Chapter VI.

19. In the absence of a court order, a non-custodial parent has no right to information about his or her child.
    FALSE.

A parent who loses custody of a child still is a parent with certain rights. Those rights include the ability to review school records and to receive unofficial copies of them, as well as to discuss the child and his or her progress with school officials. The right of access to the child is not necessarily included in non-custodial parent rights. School officials must consult the appropriate court documents granting custody to see what the custody arrangement is and whether the non-custodial parent has right of access to the child at specific times. This topic will also be discussed in greater detail in Chapter VI.

20. What one may legally do may not be the most moral or ethical action to take.
    TRUE.

Many times principals, pastors, and others have asked this author the question: *"Can I legally do this?"* when contemplating some particular action. Often, the questioner wants a simple "yes" or "no" answer, while the reality is usually a bit more complex. Just because one can legally do something does not mean it is the "right" thing to do. A pastor may certainly legally tell a principal who has served in her position for twenty years: *"Sorry. I am not renewing your contract."* But that is hardly a recommended approach. Other questions need to be asked: *"Why do you want to take this action? Has*

*the principal known you are not satisfied with her perform-
ance? Have you worked on a job improvement plan with her?"*
A twenty-year employee certainly deserves more consideration before non-renewal than does an individual who has only
been employed a year. Remembering that each of us will be
required to give an accounting of our actions at some point, the
decision-maker should ask: *"What is the right action to take?
Looking at what the law allows and the Gospel demands, what
should I do?"*

The following chapters will offer an overview of the laws
impacting Catholic schools in general and a more in-depth
consideration of some of the topics mentioned above.

CHAPTER TWO

CIVIL LAW AFFECTING CATHOLIC EDUCATION: HOW DID WE GET WHERE WE ARE?

In a text written for the National Catholic Educational Association in the 1980s, this author stated: "Private school law is a legal infant." Over twenty years later, the statement is no longer accurate. Private school law, in particular as it applies to Catholic schools, is no longer even a "legal teenager." It is an adult that has come of age.

Laws affecting Catholic education in the United States today can generally be classified in four categories: (1) constitutional law (both state and federal); (2) statutes and regulations; (3) common law principles; and (4) contract law.

Constitutional Law

Federal Constitutional law protects individuals from the arbitrary deprivation of their Constitutional freedoms by government and government officials. Constitutional law, as discussed in Chapter I, protects students and teachers in public schools, since public schools are government agencies and the administrators of public schools are public officials. Students and teachers in Catholic schools, as in all private schools, are not protected by federal Constitutional law because they are in private agencies.

Many actions, which are prohibited in public schools, are permitted in Catholic schools. For example, the First Amendment to the U.S. Constitution protects the rights of persons to free speech; hence, administrators in public schools may not prohibit the expression of an unpopular political viewpoint simply because it is unpopular. Since no such protection exists in the Catholic school, administrators can restrict both student and teacher speech. For example, any discussion supporting a woman's right to have an abortion could be forbidden in a Catholic school.

State constitutional law may apply to private as well as public schools. It is not unheard of for a state constitution to contain a statement such as: *"Anyone operating an educational institution in this state shall...."* So long as whatever is required does not unfairly constrain the rights of Catholic schools and can be shown to have some legitimate educational purpose, Catholic schools can be compelled to comply.

Statutes and Regulations

Federal and state statutes and regulations govern the public school and may govern the Catholic school as well. Failure to comply with reasonable regulations can result in the imposition of sanctions. The 1983 case of *Bob Jones v. United States* illustrates this. When Bob Jones University was found to use racially discriminatory admissions and disciplinary policies, the Internal Revenue Service withdrew the university's tax-exempt status based on a 1970 regulation proscribing the granting of tax-exempt status to any institution that discriminated on the basis of race. Before a Catholic school will be forced to comply with a law or regulation, the state must demonstrate a *compelling interest* in the enforcement of the regulations. Black defines compelling interest as: *"Term used to uphold state action in the face of attack, grounded on Equal Protection or First Amendment rights because of serious need for such state action."* (p. 256)

In *Bob Jones*, the government's compelling interest in racial equality was sufficient for the court to order the university to comply with the anti-discrimination laws or lose its tax-exempt status. The university chose to relinquish the tax-exempt status.

Other examples of compelling state interests in educational regulations might be curriculum or graduation requirements, as well as teacher certification regulations. In these cases, the state could very possibly prove a compelling state interest in the proper education of the public. However, the state cannot pass laws so restrictive that a school's very existence is placed in jeopardy.

The third type of law, which applies to both the public and private sector, is common law, which can be defined as:

> Common law is the general universal law of the land. This law is not derived from STATUTES, but is developed through court decisions over hundreds of years. Common law prevails in England and in the United States and is the controlling law unless abrogated or modified by state or federal statutes. It should be noted that common law may also be abrogated or modified by a constitutional amendment or decision by a higher court which adjudicates a constitutional issue. (Gatti and Gatti, p. 89)

Common law principles may also be considered to be derived from God's law and/or such precepts as the Golden Rule. Many common law principles may be reflected in basic morality such as that found in the Ten Commandments and in other religious writings.

Prior judicial decisions comprise an important part of common law. These decisions are often referred to as "precedents." When a lawsuit is begun, attorneys on both sides begin searching for precedents, i.e., prior cases that will support their arguments. In the United States, these prior decisions can be found in courts of record from the beginnings of this country. The United States system of common law also embraces all English cases prior to the establishment of the United States. Thus it is not unusual to find old English cases cited in modern cases.

Contract Law

The fourth type of law governing both public and private school cases is contract law. Public schools are governed by contract law in some instances, especially in the area of teacher contracts. Courts can construe faculty handbooks as part of the teacher's contract with the school. However, most cases involving public school teacher contracts also allege violation of Constitutionally-protected interests as well, so contract law is not the only applicable law.

In the Catholic school, contract law is the predominant governing law. A contract may be defined as: *"An agreement between two or more persons which creates an obligation to do or not to do a particular thing"* (Black, pp. 291-92.) Generally, the five basic elements of a contract are considered to be: (1) mutual assent (2) by legally competent parties for (3) consideration (4) to subject matter that is legal and (5) in a form of agreement which is legal.

Mutual assent implies that two parties entering into a contract agree to its provisions. A Catholic school agrees to provide an education to a student and, in return, parents accept that offer. Traditional contract law teaches that a contract will only be considered a true instrument if there has been both an offer by the first party and an acceptance of the same by the second party.

Consideration is what the first party agrees to do for the other party in exchange for something from the second party. The school accepts a student and the parents agree to pay tuition and obey the rules; a Catholic school offers a teacher a contract at a given salary and the teacher accepts the offer and agrees to perform the service. Each party to a contract receives a *benefit* and each incurs a *detriment* such as time commitment, etc. If there is no mutual "give and take," a contract does not exist.

Legally competent parties means that the parties entering into the contract are lawfully qualified to enter into the agreement. *Legal subject matter* assumes that the provisions of the contract are legal. *Legal form* may vary from state to state or from school system to school system.

Historical Development

The law relating to public schools has been in an almost constant state of development since 1960, but there were relatively few private school cases prior to the 1980s. Private school cases increase each year. In more recent times, particularly in light of the sexual abuse scandal in the Church, the marked judicial reluctance to decide cases that may involve churches and institutions sponsored by churches has largely disappeared. The sole exception would be cases that are asked to decide purely religious matters such as whether an individual is still a member in good standing of a given religious denomination.

It is significant, however, that the United States Supreme Court has never heard a private school case involving student dismissal. *Rendell-Baker v. Kohn* was a 1982 U.S. Supreme Court case that involved private school teacher dismissal and remains the only such case involving private elementary or secondary schools in history. Since case law for private higher education developed more rapidly than did the case law for private elementary and secondary schools, the body of law affecting private higher education is slightly larger than that affecting private elementary and secondary education. Private higher education law helped to establish legal principles that guide elementary and secondary legal decisions today.

It is useful to consider the parameters of public school law as one attempts to understand private school law, the law that impacts Catholic education. Prior to 1960, courts were reluctant to interfere in public school cases to any great degree. Practicing the doctrine of judicial restraint, courts decided very few cases against the institution. The legal doctrine of *in loco parentis* held that schools, colleges, and their administrators acted *in the place of parents.* In theory, if a court determined that a reasonable parent *could* (not *would*) make a decision similar to the one made by school officials, that court would find in favor of the institution. Courts generally allowed school officials to discipline students and to dismiss them without even telling the students the reasons for their actions. (See *Anthony v. Syracuse University* (1928); *Curry v. Lasell Seminary Co.,* (1897), *Gott v. Berea College* (1913), and *Stetson University v. Hunt 88* (1924.)

The landmark public university case, *Dixon v. Alabama* (1961), broke judicial restraint and won procedural due process for public college students. A student must be told what the charges are (given notice); must be allowed a hearing at which the student can present his or her side of the story; and the hearing must be before an impartial tribunal, with school officials considered impartial.

By 1974, public secondary and elementary students had firmly established their rights. The 1969 landmark case, *Tinker v. Des Moines Independent School District,* involved public elementary and secondary students who wore black armbands to protest the Vietnam War. After refusing to obey the principal's directive to remove the armbands because of a possible disruptive effect, the students were suspended. The students sued, citing a violation of their First Amendment rights to freedom of speech. The United States Supreme Court agreed with the students and held: *"It can hardly be argued that either students or teachers shed their constitutional rights to freedom of speech or expression at the [public] schoolhouse gate."* (p. 506) The First and Fourteenth Amendments' protections were thus extended to public school students facing suspension and/or expulsion. For the first time, persons under the age of eighteen were considered persons under the Constitution. Previous decisions, relying on principles of English common law, viewed children as property.

In 1975, the United States Supreme Court heard the public

school case of *Goss v. Lopez*, which involved high school students suspended for a minimum of two weeks without any kind of Constitutional due process. The Supreme Court held that such action was not "a minimal disruption" of the educational process and that students' Fifth Amendment substantive and procedural due process rights had to be protected. *Tinker* had already established that public school students have Constitutional rights that cannot be arbitrarily violated. *Goss v. Lopez* and its progeny established the tenets of Constitutional due process rights in public schools.

Wood v. Strickland, heard the same day as *Goss*, established the fact that, although public school students do not have an absolute right to an education no matter what they do, they cannot be deprived of an education without procedural due process. *Wood v. Strickland* is perhaps best known for its finding that school officials could not claim immunity from prosecution for violation of student rights if they knew or should have known the right procedures or if they acted out of malice.

Substantive due process is often defined as any property that is or can be the subject of ownership. One noted legal scholar, Kern Alexander, offered a definition in 1980 that remains a good statement of the law today: *"Substantive due process means that, 'If a state is going to deprive a person of his life, liberty or property, the state must have a valid objective and the means used must be reasonably calculated to achieve the objective'"* (p. 343). Substantive due process can also be defined as fundamental reasonableness or fairness. Substantive due process involves moral as well as legal ramifications: is this action fair and reasonable? Substantive due process applies wherever *property* or *liberty* interests can be demonstrated.

Property interest has been defined as

[t]hat which is peculiar or proper to any person; that which belongs exclusively to one.... The word is also commonly used to denote everything which is the

subject of ownership, corporeal or incorporeal, tangible or intangible, real or personal... and includes every invasion of one's property rights by actionable wrong. (Black, 1216)

It is important to note that the object owned does not have to be tangible; it can be intangible, such as the right to a public education or the right to tenure in a public institution. A liberty interest is held in Constitutional rights and in certain rights conferred by state laws. Liberty interest is sometimes defined so as to include the right to reputation. Certain conditions must be met, however, before a property interest such as tenure can be advanced. A litigant has to be able to prove that he or she has a particular right before the court can uphold that right and before any administrator can be held responsible for protecting the right; he or she must demonstrate that he or she would have been rehired if the Constitutionally protected activity had not occurred.

Teachers and other employees in the public sector may not be disciplined without Constitutional due process of law. Procedural due process consists of nine elements, the first three of which mentioned above also constitute "fairness" in the private sector:

(1) notice – the person is told exactly what he/she is accused of doing or not doing;

(2) hearing – the person is allowed to present his/her side of the "story;"

(3) before an impartial tribunal-the person tells the story to an individual or group that is impartial, not biased;

(4) the right to confront one's accusers;

(5) the right to cross-examine (question) one's accusers;

(6) the right to call witnesses on one's own behalf;

(7) the right to be represented by legal counsel;

(8) the right to a transcript of the hearing and

(9) the right to an appeal.

A public school student or teacher facing suspension or dismissal has the right to demand these protections. Obviously, the provision of such protections can be quite time and labor intensive.

Court decisions have indicated that, while Catholic schools are not bound to protect the Constitutional rights of students and employees, they are required to treat persons fairly and to observe the legal requirements of good faith and fair dealing which bind all persons in their interactions with others. Meeting these requirements constitutes reasonable due process in the private sector.

No Constitutional protections existed in the past or exist now for those in private educational institutions. The Constitution is concerned with what the government can and cannot do, not with what private entities can do. Since the Catholic school is not an extension of the state, students and teachers cannot generally claim Constitutional protections. Although well-established by law, this reality is not commonly known. However, the fact that the rules are very different in the public and private sectors provides the foundation for understanding civil law affecting education.

Catholic educational administrators can prohibit behaviors that the public school cannot prohibit. For example, a Catholic school or religious education administrator can forbid the wearing of objectionable items or the writing of materials that espouse beliefs, such as pro-choice or euthanasia positions, because such positions are contrary to the teachings of the Catholic Church. A public institutional administrator could not prohibit such actions, because the right to take such action is protected by the First Amendment of the Constitution, and affirmed by the *Tinker* court.

In early rulings the doctrine of separation of church and state has protected church-sponsored schools from being sued successfully. The last twenty-five years have seen a rise in the number of cases brought by private schools students and teachers. The last few years have witnessed an alarming number of lawsuits alleging clergy sexual abuse. The reticence that once seemed to preclude a church member suing a church authority has disappeared.

The Right of Catholic Schools to Exist

The rights of Catholic schools to exist and of parents to send their children to private schools were established by the 1925 landmark case of *Pierce v. Society of Sisters*:

> The fundamental theory of liberty upon which all governments in this Union repose excludes any general power of the State to standardize its children by forcing them to accept instruction from public teachers only. The child is not the mere creature of the State; those who nurture him and direct his destiny have the right, coupled with the high duty, to recognize and prepare him for additional obligations. (p. 535)

To understand which rights are protected in the Catholic school and which rights are not, it is necessary to understand the public school rights, rooted in the United States Constitution, as enumerated above. Generally, there are four types of laws governing schools in the United States: (1) Constitutional law, which applies almost exclusively to the public sector; (2) state and administrative regulations; (3) common law; and, (4) contract law. The latter three types govern both public and private education. Contract law is the major source of the law affecting private institutions.

State Action: the Deciding Factor in Private Education Cases

Before a Catholic school or any private institution can be required to grant Constitutional protections to teachers and/or students, the substantial presence of state action must be demonstrated. The court must determine that the state is significantly involved in a specific contested private action to such an extent that the action can fairly be said to be that of the state.

Generally, there are four theories advanced to prove state action in a private school: the presence of state funds, the exercise of state control in a contested activity, the tax-exempt status of the private institution, and the public function or benefit theory that holds that if an institution performs a public function, such as education, the private institution can be held to the same standards. The public function theory has been virtually abandoned in legal decisions.

Historically, there are three cases involving private schools, two of which involve Catholic schools that provide much of the foundation for legal decisions today. The first case was the 1970 case, *Bright v. Isenbarger*, in which dismissed students alleged that state action was present because of state regulation of the school and the school's tax-exempt status. The court rejected the claim: *"Accordingly... this court holds that because the State of Indiana was in no way involved in the challenged actions, defendants' expulsion of plaintiffs was not state action."* (p. 1395)

The facts of *Bright* are as follow. Two students were dismissed for the remainder of the school year for a second violation of a rule forbidding visits to a nearby public school. The students maintained that since the school was certified by the state of Indiana, was governed by state school law, and received state and federal grant monies, that the state action requirement was met and, therefore, Constitutional rights were theirs. The court disagreed, holding as stated above, that the state has to be somehow involved in the actual decision resulting in the expulsion. Since there was no evidence that the state had anything at all to do with the disciplinary actions of the school, state action could not be found and no Constitutional rights existed.

In a 1976 expulsion case, *Wisch v. Sanford School, Inc.*,

a student maintained that the federal funding present in the private school through various governmental programs constituted state action. The court, however, disagreed:

> Plaintiff must show that there was more than "some" state action in this case; not every involvement by the state in the affairs of a private individual or organization, whether through funding or regulation, may be used as a basis for a [Section] 1983 or Fourteenth Amendment claim. The involvement must be "substantial." (p. 1313)

In a 1979 case, an expelled student and his father brought suit against a Catholic high school in *Geraci v. St. Xavier High School* and alleged the presence of state action. Once again the court found that, even if state action were present, it would have to be so entwined with the contested activity, dismissal of the student, that a symbiotic relationship could be held to exist between the state and the school's dismissal of the student. If no such relationship can be established, state action is not present and Constitutional protections do not apply:

> [O]ther than ascertaining that the school meets minimum state standards for a high school, the state exercises no control over the school whatsoever. This is certainly not the sort of pervasive state involvement required for a finding of symbiotic state action. (p. 148)

The one case involving a private school teacher contesting dismissal was heard by the United States Supreme Court in 1982, *Rendell-Baker v. Kohn*. This case is significant because, although the school received over 90% of its funds from the state, the Supreme Court declined to find the presence of state action significant enough to warrant Constitutional protections. Previous lower court decisions had suggested the difficulty of proving significant state action present in teacher dismissals in the private school.

Rendell-Baker indicates that, unless the state can somehow be shown to be involved in the contested activity, the court will not intervene in the action. Thus, it seems that the state action argument is useless when a Catholic school student or teacher attempts to claim Constitutional protections in the private setting.

Breach of Contract

Most cases involving teacher or student dismissal from Catholic schools allege contract violations. The remedy for breach of contract is damages, not reinstatement. Breach of contract can be defined as occurring "when a party does not perform that which he or she was under an absolute duty to perform and the circumstances are such that his or her failure was neither justified nor excused." (Gatti and Gatti, p. 124) A contract is the legal agreement of two parties to each perform some action or refrain from some action for the other. Whatever the parties agree to do or not do is called "consideration." A Catholic school provides an education for a parent's child (agrees to do something) and receives tuition from the parent (gets a benefit). Increasingly, Catholic school handbooks contain a provision requiring parents to sign a statement that they agree to be contractually bound by the handbook's regulations as a condition of their children's enrollment in the school.

The old, but still very relevant, 1973 case, *Weithoff v. St. Veronica's School*, is an example of breach of contract. A teacher was dismissed for marrying a priest who had not been laicized and she incurred the penalty, which was Church practice at the time, of excommunication from the Church. It is easy to understand why such an individual might be considered unfit to teach in a Catholic school. However, the teacher had signed a contract binding her to the "promulgated policies" of the parish. The parish school board had enacted a policy requiring all teachers to be practicing Catholics. The policy, however, was kept in the secretary's files and never promulgated to the teachers. The court found for the teacher because the school did not meet its obligation of promulgation.

In a more recent case, *Little v. St. Mary Magdalene*, the court ruled that a non-Catholic teacher in a Catholic school who had signed an agreement containing a "cardinal's clause," requiring her to live a life consistent with the teachings of the Catholic Church, violated that agreement when she contracted a marriage with a divorced Catholic who had not yet received an annulment, even though such a marriage was perfectly acceptable in the teacher's religion.

Little and *Weithoff* illustrate that the courts will look to the provisions of contracts in breach of contract cases and will base decisions on what the parties involved have agreed to do, not on what they should have agreed to do or on any other factor. Courts have upheld the right of private schools to make rules of conduct for teachers and students that would not be permitted in public institutions. However, the private school must have policies that prohibit certain types of conduct before it can dismiss a teacher for misconduct.

The case of *Holy Name School of the Congregation of the Holy Name of Jesus of Kimberly v. Dept. of Industry, Labor and Human Relations, and Mary P. Retlick* illustrates this. Retlick's contract was not renewed because she married a divorced Catholic man who had not obtained an annulment of his first marriage. The school sought to prove that she was not entitled to unemployment benefits because she willfully violated her contract. Retlick, however, was able to demonstrate that the only policy the school had regarding divorced and remarried teachers concerned religion teachers. Further, the principal had encouraged the teacher to live with the man rather than marry him if she could not marry within the Church, so the school's defense that the marriage was immoral could not withstand judicial scrutiny. Retlick received unemployment.

Courts will consider the characteristics and behavior of the parties involved in a contract. Just as the principal's behavior in *Holy Names* discredited the allegation of immoral behavior in the teacher's action, in a different case a teacher's behavior led the court to find that the teacher should have known that his conduct did not meet the norms of the sponsoring school. In the Louisiana case, *Bischoff v. Brothers of the Sacred Heart*, a former Catholic seminarian, who had been twice divorced and remarried without the appropriate annulments, was held to have been responsible for knowing what the school required. Once the school learned of his marriages, the school rescinded its contract, and Mr. Bischoff sued. The court ruled: *"Plaintiff testified he was aware of Catholic dogma regarding divorce and we conclude, as did the Trial Jury, that the plaintiff's bad faith caused error and the contract was void ab initio."* (p. 151)

Historically, courts have been reluctant to intervene in disputes involving church-related schools and programs because of the separation of church and state. The New Hampshire case of *Reardon et al. v. LeMoyne et al.* drew much attention from the public and the press because it involved four Roman Catholic sisters whose contracts were not renewed after five to twelve years of employment. The sisters sued the parish school board, the superintendent of schools, and the bishop. The sisters alleged that their contracts had been violated. They had signed the same employment contracts as had lay personnel and statements in the contract and in the school's handbook gave a dismissed teacher the right of a hearing and an appeal. At the direction of the superintendent, the sisters were not allowed a hearing. The trial court declined to intervene, holding that such intervention would be a violation of separation of church and state. On appeal, the state supreme court ruled that a court could intervene in non-doctrinal contract disputes and ruled in favor of the sisters who were not reinstated. An out-of-court settlement was negotiated.

The crux of the *Reardon* problem seemed to be the language of the employment contract. The language was, at best, ambiguous: one clause indicated that it would terminate at the end of the contractual year; another clause, clearly contradicting the first clause, stated that retirement of the employee was to occur at the end of the school year during which the employee attained his or her seventieth birthday. The policies also stated that if a contract was not to be renewed, the employee was to be notified in writing and given well-documented reasons for the non-renewal. The contract contained a further provision allowing appeal to the diocesan school board. The sisters then went to court asking the court to construe their employment contracts. The trial court found that the court could only exercise jurisdiction over the lay members of the school board and not over the superintendent and the bishop because of separation of church and state. The trial court also stated that the plaintiffs would not prevail against the school board.

On appeal, the state supreme court found that the doctrine of separation of church and state did not preclude jurisdiction in non-doctrinal contract matters:

> Religious entities, however, are not totally immune from responsibility under civil law. In religious controversies involving property or contractual rights outside the doctrinal realm, a court may accept jurisdiction and render a decision without violating the first amendment.... It is clear from the foregoing discussion that civil courts are permitted to consider the validity of non-doctrinal claims which are raised by parties to contracts with religious entities. This requires the courts to evaluate the pertinent contractual provisions and extrinsic evidence to determine whether any violations of the contract have occurred, and to order appropriate remedies, if necessary. (pp. 431-32)

In essence, the state supreme court found that the trial court should have accepted jurisdiction over the bishop and the superintendent as well as over the school board members. Further, the state supreme court held that the trial court should have ruled on the requests made by the sisters and should have analyzed their legal rights.

Reardon illustrates the extreme importance of contract language. One cannot allow anyone, including members of a religious congregation, to sign an employment contract and then not expect to be held to the provisions of that contract. The school board should have granted the sisters a hearing because that is what the contract said the board would do when it was requested to do so.

The above cases involving church schools illustrate that administrators cannot hide behind the First Amendment as a cover for any actions they wish to take. The courts have made it clear that they do have jurisdiction over the non-doctrinal elements of a contract made with a religious entity.

The *Holy Names* case illustrates that, while courts will not rule on the rightness or wrongness of a given religious doctrine, they will look to see whether the action based on the doctrine is reasonable and consistent. The *Weithoff* case illustrates the need for clear polices that are disseminated to all. The *Dolter* case established the right of the courts to intervene in sex discrimination cases. These cases helped to establish the fact that persons in the private sector do have rights that will be protected by the courts. Administrators are required to know what those rights are and to provide protection. The *Little* case demonstrates that Catholic schools have the right to hold people to behavioral regulations based on religion, even if an individual's personal religious beliefs would permit the behavior. Legally sound written policies and guidelines greatly facilitate both the knowledge and protection of the rights of all.

Recent Student Discipline Case
Alleging Breach of Contract

A July 15, 2004 opinion from the Rhode Island Supreme Court, *Russell Gorman, Jr. et al. v. St. Raphael Academy*, a case alleging breach of contract in a student discipline dispute, represents a victory for all Catholic schools. The decision clearly supports the right of Catholic schools and programs to establish reasonable rules and regulations. The *Gorman* court ruled that courts have no right to interfere in private school disciplinary regulations unless they violate law or public policy. Because this case is recent and pivotal, a comprehensive discussion follows.

The Facts

Russell Gorman, Jr., entered St. Raphael Academy in Pawtucket, Rhode Island, in the Fall of 2001. Russell wore his hair six to eight inches below the shirt collar in the back. Shortly after the beginning of his freshman year, school officials instructed him to cut his hair or face expulsion. Russell, with his parents' support, refused. The parents sought and were granted a temporary restraining order keeping the school from expelling Russell for his hair length.

The principal revised the school handbook for the 2002-2003 school year to include a new hair-length regulation stipulating that the hair of male students could be no longer than the bottom of the shirt collar. School officials testified that Russell's parents were notified of the impending rule change before the end of the school year; the parents claimed that they did not know of the change until the summer and were not given a new handbook until August of that year when they filed an amended complaint alleging breach of contract and seeking injunctive relief.

The legal arguments and decisions

The trial judge, relying on a public school case, held that the rule was arbitrary and capricious and that the school's rules had to be related to the mission of the school. In effect, the judge violated the principle of judicial restraint which holds that courts do not generally substitute their opinions for those of the professionals. St. Raphael appealed the decision, which could have had the effect of eventually making virtually every Catholic school rule subject to judicial scrutiny.

The Gormans alleged breach of contract; St. Raphael argued that they did not identify the alleged contract, its terms or breach. St. Raphael's further argued that the judge improperly placed the burden of proof on the school.

The state supreme court found that the trial judge applied equitable, rather than legal contract principles, to the claim. An equitable remedy is only available when there is no adequate remedy at law. The long-standing general principle has been that the remedy for breach of a contract for personal services (e.g., education) is damages, not reinstatement, because courts will not compel performance of such a contract if one of the parties does not wish to perform. In addition, the school argued that, since the parents did not sign the 2002-2003 contract in the school handbook, no valid contract could exist.

The trial judge suggested that the Gormans had a four-year contract for Russell's education, a suggestion that the state supreme court rejected while it held that the contract was an annual one subject to renewal.

Question of First Impression

The state supreme court opinion held that this decision was one of first impression, the first time such a conflict had been litigated. Further, the justices observed that they could find no published case in any jurisdiction that dealt with hair-length rules in private educational institutions. Thus, this decision is groundbreaking.

Contract Law Rulings

The court stated: *"Because contracts for private education have unique qualities, we must construe them in a manner that leaves the school administration broad discretion to meet its educational and doctrinal responsibilities.*" School handbooks can be considered contracts. Parents of St. Raphael's students are required to sign tuition contracts agreeing to the terms of the student handbook. Therefore, the court held that the relationship between students/parents and the school has to be a contractual one. The court held that: "*...absent a violation of law or public policy, it is not within the province of the court to inject itself in the rule-making authority of a private school.*"

The court recognized that some public school litigants have alleged that the right to wear one's hair the way one wishes is a Constitutional freedom guaranteed by the First Amendment but, following earlier federal decisions, held that a private school would have to be a state actor before it would be required to recognize constitutional rights. Therefore, no Constitutional protections exist.

Catholic schools and programs everywhere owe a debt of gratitude to St. Raphael's Academy. The willingness of the school and the diocese to fight for the right of Catholic schools to enact and enforce rules makes administration an easier task and underscores the reality that contract law, not constitutional law, governs the relationship of a Catholic school with its students.

Legal History: How does it Impact Current Case Developments?

An understanding of the historical basis for private school legal decisions is essential for administrators of Catholic schools. Today's "big" issues, while different in some ways from those of past decades, are much the same in others. A brief discussion of the most current "hot" topics in education law will be offered in subsequent chapters.

The third millennium holds new legal challenges for Catholic educators. Law is not ministry, but it is a boundary around ministry. So long as educators keep within the confines of the law, they can do whatever they wish in ministry. Moving outside the boundary can cause legal problems. The law is, at its core, based on common sense. The following chapters will attempt to discuss the common sense implications of legal issues important for today's Catholic educators.

CHAPTER THREE

TORTS: WHAT DOES THE EDUCATOR NEED TO KNOW?

The last chapter discussed the sources of the law affecting education in the United States. This chapter will discuss tort law, with a special emphasis on negligence. Tort cases, some of the most common types of legal action brought under statutory and regulatory law, are the ones most frequently brought against educators. Knowledge of torts and the kinds of cases that can arise should provide educators with the preventive knowledge needed to *"stay out of court."*

A tort, according to Black, is *"a private or civil wrong or injury... for which the court will provide a remedy in the form of an action for damages."* (p. 1489) Historically, torts are generally classified in education law in four categories: corporal punishment, search and seizure, defamation, and negligence. Many of the relatively new causes of action being brought in such areas as confidentiality, boundaries, harassment, and related issues are also negligence cases. Since negligence is the most often litigated tort, it will be considered last in this chapter. It should be noted that the law governing torts is virtually the same in both the public and private sectors.

Corporal Punishment and other Types of Abuse

Corporal punishment is less an issue today than it was in 1977, when in *Ingraham v. Wright* the U.S. Supreme Court ruled that students in public schools do not have the protection of the Eighth Amendment when subjected to corporal punishment, even if the punishment can be considered "cruel and unusual." In 1984, very few states outlawed corporal punishment in schools; today the majority of states forbid its use. New areas of concern have surfaced in more recent times. The concept of corporal punishment has been enlarged to include any bodily touching that can be construed as punitive. A related issue is that of mental or emotional abuse. Claims of mental abuse do not seem to have received serious consideration in the 1970's and 80's; today, it is not uncommon for teachers to be accused of mental abuse or for teachers to hear reports of mental abuse from their students. How then is a teacher to know what to report?

The majority of cases will probably not be clear-cut, and an educator may well struggle to decide if a report should be made. Many law enforcement officials and some attorneys instruct educators to report everything that students tell them that could possibly constitute abuse or negligence. They further caution teachers and other adults that it is not their job to determine if abuse has occurred. As a mandated reporter, the teacher has a responsibility to present the information to the agency designated to receive reports. Appropriate officials will determine whether the report should be investigated further or simply "screened out" as a well-intentioned report that does not appear to be in the category of abuse.

Who Should File the Report?

In the past, it was not unusual to have a school policy requiring that the principal make all child abuse and/or neglect reports, so that the same person was reporting all situations in a given school. This approach, if taken today, can be extremely problematic as states clearly require the person with the suspicion (i.e., the educator or staff member) to file the report. The staff member must personally report abuse to the appropriate agency and notify the principal or other administrator. Certainly, the principal can be present when a teacher or other staff member makes a report. Additionally, all reporters should immediately inform their principals that they have made reports. It is legally dangerous for the institution when a police officer or other official appears to investigate a report of child abuse and the administrator does not know that a report has been filed.

Administrators should decide in advance how visits and requests from police or social workers will be handled. States now require that school personnel allow officials to examine and question students. Administrators, counselors, or teachers may request to remain with the student while he or she meets with police or social workers, but the investigating official has the right to refuse to allow school personnel to be present.

How Can A School Protect Its Students?

It is a well-established reality that schools and churches can attract persons with abusive tendencies who are seeking children upon whom to prey. Thus officials must do everything in their power to investigate the backgrounds of persons before employment. Chapter I contains a discussion of some points to consider in background checks.

Any student or parent complaint alleging child abuse by a teacher or other staff member must receive serious attention. Failure to do so can put the institution and its officials at grave legal risk. Administrators and school boards should adopt policies governing reporting child abuse/neglect by staff *before* the need for such policies surfaces. It is preferable to have a policy that is never needed than to have no policy and be forced to try to construct one when faced with a need.

Search and Seizure

Search and seizure problems occur when a student alleges injury from a search of person or property. Early cases delineated differences between probable and reasonable cause. Probable cause is a stricter standard than reasonable cause and will be held to exist when a school official has reliable knowledge about the whereabouts of dangerous or potentially dangerous material on campus. Reasonable cause is a suspicion with some basis in fact. A phone call, a note, or a suspicious appearance can comprise reasonable cause.

Historically, case law indicated that once a public school administrator involves the police in a search or turns seized items over to the police, Fourth Amendment protections do apply and improperly-seized evidence can be excluded from a trial if criminal convictions are later sought. Thus, an improper search could be a violation of a student's constitutional rights and administrators can be held liable for damages as perpetrators of constitutional torts. However, a rationale for holding public school administrators to a less strict standard than other public officials to in search and seizure situations was primarily based on the *in loco parentis* doctrine: school officials have the right to act as a reasonable parent could if he or she suspected a child to be in possession of some illegal or dangerous substance.

Catholic educators could be subject to private tort suits if a student claims to have been harmed by a search. Like public school officials, private educators could be charged with the torts of assault and battery and/or invasion of privacy. The search's level of intrusion determines the court's degree of scrutiny. Asking a student to empty his pockets would require a less strict degree of scrutiny than would a body search.

If You Have To Do It, How Should You Do It?

Many educators are reviewing the need for policies and procedures regarding student searches. In 1985, the U.S. Supreme Court ruled in *New Jersey v. T.L.O.* that public school administrators did not need search warrants or probable cause to search students and their belongings. Probable cause is a stricter standard than reasonable cause and exists when a school official has reliable knowledge about the whereabouts of dangerous or potentially dangerous material on campus. Reasonable cause is a suspicion with some basis in fact. A phone call, a note, or a suspicious appearance can constitute reasonable cause.

The Catholic educator, obviously, is not bound to Fourth Amendment search and seizure requirements. However, as indicated above, schools could be subject to suits for damages if a student alleges harm as a result of an unreasonable search. Common sense precautions are in order. Teachers and other staff members should be given guidelines for any search of student belongings or students themselves. Procedures for searching students should be more stringent than those for searching mere possessions. Strip searches should never be permitted.

School property does not belong to the student. Schools and programs strengthen their legal positions by including a policy in the parent/student handbook that states: *"The school is co-tenant of lockers and desks and reserves the right to search them at any time without notice."*

Some suggested guidelines for search and seizure protocols follow.

General Considerations

1. Ask yourself if what you are looking for is worth the search. Looking for a lost dollar bill is generally not worth the effort beyond a general question: *"Has anyone seen Tommy's dollar?"*

2. Ask everyone to search around desks/lockers/in personal items. Approach is everything. A teacher might say: *"Let's all look in our pockets and see if Mary's ring might have fallen in"* (as teacher looks in his/her pockets). In a secondary school setting, a teacher might say: *"Mary has lost her ring. Does anyone have any idea where it might be? Could you look in your belongings to see if it may have ended up with your things by mistake?"* The teacher can then deal with the student who has the item, but the approach is non-accusatory.

3. Have another staff member present in any searches of individual students or property.

Searching Lockers & Desks
1. Ask the student if there is anything he/she wishes to show you.
2. Ask the student to remove the items from the desk and open any item you direct him/her to open.
3. Put any contraband in a separate container (if it will fit). Have the student sign a statement that the items were found in the locker/desk. Take items to the office where the administrator can "take over," talk with the student and contact parents, if necessary.
4. If there is nothing "illegal" in the desk or locker, thank the student for his/her cooperation and state that you are glad that the matter has been resolved (in age appropriate language, of course).

Searching Students & Purses/Coats/ Book Bags (which can be considered extensions of the person)
1. Ask the student if you may search his/her pockets, coat, book bag or purse.
2. If the answer is yes, ask the student to take everything out and show it to you.
3. If the answer is no, isolate the student and the purse or bag under an adult's supervision.
4. Call the parent, explain the situation, tell the parent you would like to clear the student's name and ask him/her to either tell the student to cooperate or to come to school and conduct the search him/herself. If the parent refuses, tell the parent that the school/parental partnership is broken and that arrangements will have to be made to transfer the student to another school.

If the police Ask to Search a Student:
1. Ask for the officer's identification.
2. Ask if the officer has a warrant. If he/she has one, let the officer proceed. If there is no warrant, politely

tell the officer that once one is obtained and presented, you will make the student available for a search. Exception: if a clear threat to health or safety is involved, use your best judgment.

Administrators should not hesitate to consult police officers and attorneys when needed. When controversy arises, the best defense is having followed clear policies and procedures.

Defamation

Defamation is the violation of a person's liberty interest or right to reputation. Defamation is the utterance of words in spoken or written form that are detrimental to the subject's reputation. Defamation can encompass a wide range of remarks; almost anything negative said about someone could be construed as defamatory since it could affect a person's reputation or the esteem in which others hold the person.

The potential for defamation to be alleged certainly exists in administrators' relationships with students and teachers. Administrators should be factual in their comments, whether written or oral, about the conduct of teachers or students. The news media report defamation cases in which the defendant asserts an affirmative defense of truth. School officials are often held to a higher standard than are average persons because school officials hold a position of trust. Thus damage to reputation, rather than the truth of the allegation, can determine the outcome.

Privacy and reputation are two serious legal issues facing Catholic educators today. Both students and staff members expect that information concerning them will be revealed only to those with a right to know. Policies should require the use of reasonable measures to safeguard private information.

Defamation, then, is an unprivileged communication that harms the reputation of another. Defamation, which may involve invasion of privacy, can be either spoken, *slander*, or written, *libel*.

All members of the educational community should be concerned with protecting the reputations of all in their schools. Educators should exercise great care in keeping student and teacher records, as well as in speaking about students and behavior. It is only just that all involved in the educational ministry of the school refrain from gossip or unnecessary derogatory remarks about any members of the school community. The best advice for everyone is to be as factual as possible in official documents and to refrain from "editorial" comments.

It is more professional, and legally more appropriate, to write: *"Bob has been absent four times this month, late for class eight times, and sent to the assistant principal's office for disrupting class three times,"* than to write: *"Bobby is absent too much, late most of the time, and always in trouble."* It is better to write: *"Susan is reading on a first-grade level,"* than to write, *"Susan can't read."*

Student files present special problems. Past practices often included using student folders as a collection place for any and all items. It was, and in some cases still is, the norm to find absentee notes, student papers, old academic, non-standardized tests, and the like in a student's file. The best approach to file safety is to limit the contents of official files to the following: (1) academic transcripts; (2) standardized test results; (3) health form(s); and, (4) emergency sheets. Everything else can and should be stored elsewhere. If there is no reason to have an item in a student's file, it should be stored elsewhere. Disciplinary records, in particular, should not be stored in official files. Students are still in a formative stage, and educators should exercise extreme caution in storing information that could be harmful to a student. Disciplinary records should not be a part of the information sent to another institution when a student transfers or graduates. If the new school requires disciplinary information, the transferring school's administrator(s) should consider preparing a document containing the information and having the parents sign a statement that they have seen the document and agree to its being sent.

Writing Recommendations: a Possible Legal Minefield?

In today's litigious society, most educators are familiar with the problems of writing legally non-controversial recommendations without sacrificing the truth. Further, most people have read recommendations that seem to say very little. All educators must understand that no one has an absolute, legal right to a recommendation. Fairness, however, would seem to indicate that only the most extreme situations should result in a student's being denied a recommendation. High school and college recommendations pose particular problems. For example, a student or parent may demand a recommendation from a certain teacher if the recommendation must come from a teacher in a given discipline. If a teacher were to decline to write the recommendation, the parent would probably simply complain to the principal and/or guidance counselor and the teacher may become embroiled in a dispute in which there are no winners.

Students can request and receive letters verifying enrollment, and factual statements can be made about education and participation in extra-curricular activities. The guideline is to be as fair as possible. School officials should strive to be just and respectful of the dignity of others in all communications, whether official or not, and to say only what can be shown to have some valid relationship to the professional situation. In so doing, educators protect themselves against possible lawsuits alleging defamation and/or invasion of privacy.

Confidentiality of Records

An issue related to invasion of privacy is confidentiality of records. If administrators follow the procedures outlined above, the risk of having problematic materials in student files becomes minimal.

The contents of student files should be released only to authorized persons. Even faculty and staff member should have access to student files only for appropriate, education-related reasons. Parental signatures should be required before records are sent to anyone.

Many persons associated with Catholic schools can recall when neither they nor students' parents were permitted access to student records. Congress passed the Buckley Amendment, granting students and parents the right to inspect school records, in 1975. It should be noted that there are some legal experts who believe that the Buckley Amendment does not apply to private schools. The amendment contains a clause stating that the legislation does not apply to private schools *solely* because of the presence of government funds (e.g., federal commodities in cafeterias, bloc grant money, etc.). However, this belief has never been tested in court.

There are cases in which private sector officials have been required to comply with federal legislation, such as anti-discrimination statutes. The requirement was based on public policy considerations and commonly accepted standards of behavior. It is better to comply *voluntarily* with legislation, such as the Buckley Amendment, than to risk becoming a test case for the courts. Legalities aside, it seems only right that persons affected by records have the right to see them.

Negligence

Negligence, the most common tort, is *"the unintentional doing or not doing of something which wrongfully causes injury to another"* (Gatti and Gatti, p. 246). Case law indicates that teachers and administrators are expected to act as reasonable persons; when their action or lack of action results in injury to a student, a finding of negligence can be made. There are four elements which must be present before negligence can exist. These elements defined by many legal writers are: duty, violation of duty, proximate cause, and injury. If any one of the four elements is missing, no legal negligence and hence, no tort can be found to exist. Since negligence is the unintentional act which results in an injury, a person charged with negligence is generally not going to face criminal charges or spend time in prison.

An understanding of each of the four elements necessary to constitute a finding of negligence is essential for today's educator. Previous defenses such as charitable immunity, an institution doing a charitable work is immune from liability for negligence, are no longer available. Every Catholic educator should know that the days of people being unwilling to sue the church and its programs are over; litigants and lawyers often view the church as a wealthy, desirable defendant able to pay large sums in damages.

The first element is *duty*. The person charged with negligence must have had a duty in the situation. Students have a right to safety and teachers and administrators have a responsibility to protect the safety of all those entrusted to their care. Teachers have a duty to provide reasonable supervision of their students. Administrators must have developed rules and regulations which provide for safety. Teachers will generally not be held responsible for injuries occurring at a place where, or at a time when, they had no responsibility. A student injured on the way to school, for example, will not be able to prove that school officials had a duty to protect him or her.

Administrators must be aware that simply stating that the school does not accept a given responsibility does not necessarily mean that the school has no responsibility. One example is the situation of students arriving well before the opening of school and/or staying after school when no supervision is present. Even today, many principals believe that writing a rule that states: *"There is no supervision before 7:30 a.m. or after*

3:00 p.m." absolves them from liability for any injuries students may sustain while on school property before or after school. However, over thirty years of case law indicates that administrators can be held liable for such injuries, even if there is a stated policy that no supervision will be provided.

In an old, but oft-quoted 1967 New Jersey case, *Titus v. Lindberg*, an administrator was found to be liable for a student injury occurring on school grounds before school because: he knew that students arrived on the grounds before the doors were opened; he was present on campus when students were; he had established no rules for student conduct outside the building; and he had not provided for the supervision of the students. Although the principal had notified parents that no supervision would be provided, the court found that he had a reasonable duty to provide such supervision when he knew students were on the property as a regular practice. Understandably concerned principals may ask: *"Am I expected to provide twenty-four hour supervision?"* The answer is "no." The court will look at the reasonable nature of the administrator's behavior. Probably no court would expect a supervisor to be present on school premises at 6:00 a.m.; however, the court will expect some policy as to when students may arrive, what the rules are, what kind of supervision and when it is provided, and what the penalties for non-compliance are. Many other cases followed the reasoning in *Titus*. Current law seems to be shifting much responsibility for student behavior from the parent to the school staff.

While courts tend to hold educators strictly accountable in situations in which they have duties, they are reluctant to extend that accountability to other situations. A teacher, wearing a school jacket, who is walking through a mall on Saturday afternoon does not have a duty to intervene if two students are fighting or otherwise misbehaving in the mall. One cannot be held responsible for acts occurring in a place and at a time when one has no responsibility for the persons acting.

Educators should be aware, however, that it is possible to assume a duty that one would otherwise not have. If the teacher in the above example decides to try and intervene in a fight between two of his students in the mall, he or she has assumed a duty that would not otherwise be required. Once a teacher assumes the duty, the ordinary rules of negligence will apply.

The second element that must be present for a finding of negligence is *violation of duty*. Negligence cannot exist if there has been no violation of duty. Courts expect that accidents and spontaneous actions can occur. If a teacher is properly supervising a playground and one child picks up a rock, throws it, and so injures another child, the teacher should not be held liable if the teacher had no prior knowledge that a particular student was likely to throw a rock. However, if a teacher who is supervising recess were to allow the rock-throwing to continue without attempting to stop it and a student is injured, the teacher would probably be held liable.

Courts have stopped short of requiring that teachers be physically present at all times. Courts understand that emergencies can happen that necessitate the teacher leaving a class unattended for a short period of time. But, the court will always utilize "the reasonable person" test – did the teacher act in a way that a reasonable teacher would act?

When teachers are physically present, they are also expected to be mentally present. Far too often, this author has observed students playing on a playground while the teacher supervisors, who are physically present, are engaged in conversation in a corner of the playground and are not mentally aware of what is going on around them. Recent case law suggests that mere physical presence is not enough to avoid liability if a student is injured. If a student can successfully argue that the teacher was not paying attention and that if she had been, an injury would have been prevented, the student will in all likelihood prevail.

The third requirement of negligence is that the violation of duty must be the *proximate cause* of the injury. In other words, would the injury have occurred if proper supervision had been present? The court must decide whether proper supervision could have prevented the injury. The tragic 1967 Minnesota case of *Levandoski v. Jackson City School District*, which certainly is an example of a teacher's nightmare, illustrates. A teacher failed to report that a thirteen-year-old girl was missing from class; thus, the administrators had no knowledge that the student was absent, and parents were not notified. The child's body was later found some distance from the school. The child's mother filed suit against the school district and alleged that, if the child's absence had been reported, the murder would not have happened. The court found that no evidence existed to show that if the absence had been properly reported, the murder could have been prevented. It should be easy to see how a slightly different fact pattern, such as one in which the student was found murdered on the school grounds, would have produced a finding of liability against the school. The Levandoski court simply found that, in this particular case, the violation of duty was not the proximate cause of the injury.

The well-known case of *Smith v. Archbishop of St. Louis*, involving a Catholic school, illustrates the concept of proximate cause. A second grade teacher kept a lighted candle on her desk every morning during the month of May to honor the Mother of God. She gave no special instructions to the students regarding the danger of a lighted candle. A student, dressed in an untreated crepe paper costume, walked to close to the fire and the costume caught fire. The child sustained facial and upper body burns such that during the five years the litigation was in process, she was subjected to several operations and painful treatments. She sustained psychological as well as physical injuries and competent physicians testified that she would likely experience psychological problems for the rest of her life. The Archdiocese of St. Louis appealed the holding. The appellate court upheld the award and the finding of negligent supervision against the Archdiocese. The court also discussed the concept of foreseeability, which generally holds that a person can be found negligent only if injury were foreseeable: *"To recover, plaintiff need not show that the very injury resulting from defendant's negligence was foreseeable, but merely that a reasonable person could have foreseen that injuries of the type suffered would be likely to occur under the circumstances."* (p. 521) The plaintiff did not have to prove that the defendant could foresee that a particular injury, such as crepe paper catching fire might occur; the plaintiff merely had to establish that a reasonable teacher would have foreseen that injuries could result from an unattended lighted candle in a second grade classroom when no safety instructions were given.

The fourth element of negligence is *injury*. No matter how irresponsible the behavior of a supervisor, there is no negligence if there is no injury. If a teacher were to leave twenty first-graders unsupervised near a lake and no one was injured, there can be no finding of negligence.

Most negligence cases occur in the classroom because that is where students and teachers spend most of their time. However, shop and lab classes, as well as athletic activities, carry more potential for injury. Case law indicates that courts expect supervisors to exercise greater caution in these areas than they would in ordinary classrooms.

Being Proactive: Preventing Injuries

The beginning of the academic year and regular intervals throughout the year are good times to review potential hazards and dangerous practices in the areas under one's supervision. Teachers and other staff members can contribute to the overall safety of the school by giving thought to the following questions and discussing their responses and findings with the appropriate persons.

(1) Are there any hazardous conditions in my class-room or other instructional area(s)? If yes, can I eliminate them on my own? If I cannot, do I know whom to contact and how to record the conditions and actions taken?

(2) Have I noticed any hazardous conditions in the building or on the school or parish grounds? Whom should I inform? If the condition is not corrected, then I need to document that fact and notify my superior.

(3) Have I noticed any patterns of dangerous behavior among the young people I supervise? What steps can I take to lessen, if not completely eliminate, these behaviors? Are my rules clear and consistent-ly enforced? Do I understand it is more important for students to be safe than to have their own way? If I do, do I make decisions based on student safety first?

(4) Have I ever observed suspicious persons in or around the building? Have I reported these obser-vations to my supervisor? Are signs directing visi-tors to the office clearly in evidence? Do people obey the signs?

(5) Is there any situation that makes me uncomfort-able? If yes, why am I uncomfortable? Should I discuss this with the principal? When in doubt, it is always better to err on the side of caution.

Other topics related to negligence will be discussed in subsequent chapters. The wise administrator and teacher will strive to be alert to conditions and situations that could put student safety at risk and expose the school to legal liability, and will take appropriate action as needed.

CHAPTER FOUR

BISHOPS, PASTORS, PRINCIPALS AND BOARDS: RIGHTS AND RESPONSIBILITIES

Two systems of law govern Catholic schools: the civil law of the country, state, city, etc., and canon law, the law of the Catholic Church. Civil courts, respecting the First Amendment's guarantee of the free exercise of religion, will generally not interfere in the internal affairs of religious institutions. Civil law recognizes the right of religious organizations to govern themselves. This right, however, is not absolute. Civil courts will not allow religious institutions to evade legal responsibilities by "hiding behind" church law. Within the wide parameter imposed by civil law, though, churches have significant autonomy.

Canon law governs both the existence and continuance of Catholic institutions. A school can call itself Catholic only with the approval of the bishop. The bishop has the duty to inspect schools as well as the right to appoint and remove teachers of religion. Traditionally, it has been said that all Catholic schools are subject to their bishops in matters of faith and morals and in all other matters prescribed by the Church's Code of Canon Law.

The bishop has final responsibility for all church laws in his diocese. He may, and generally does, delegate much of his power to other persons in the diocese, such as the superintendent, the vicar, diocesan boards, and similar bodies. Although he may delegate power, he can never delegate responsibility. Mirroring the civil law theory of *respondeat superior*, the bishop can be required to answer in canon law for the actions of his designates.

The canon law equivalent of a civil corporation is the "juridic person," an individual legal entity recognized by the

Church. Schools may be either separate juridic persons or part of the juridic person of another entity, such as a parish or religious congregation. Although a thorough consideration of canon law is beyond the scope of this text, it may be helpful to examine briefly the four most common types of Catholic schools operating in the country today.

The first type is the parish elementary or high school that operates as part of a parish governed by a pastor who is the ultimate authority in the parish, subject only to the bishop. It is important for everyone associated with a Catholic school to understand that its governance is not a democracy. As the bishop has the final responsibility for the diocese, the pastor has the final responsibility for the parish, limited only by the bishop's right to review. The pastor probably shares his decision-making with many persons and entities in the parish. One would hope that he operates in a collegial spirit. However, he stands alone in a very sense under canon law in his ultimate responsibility for the decisions that guide the life of his parish and the school.

More recently, changing demographics and declining enrollments in some dioceses, as well as strategic planning efforts, have resulted in the development of the regional school, often a consolidation of two or more schools. Governance structures may take different forms in these schools. In some, one pastor, or an individual designated by the bishop as the parochial vicar, may have the final responsibility; in others, there may be a shared decision-making structure among the pastors of the parishes supporting the school.

A third type of school, the diocesan school, has long been associated with secondary education. In more recent times, some dioceses have begun to sponsor diocesan regional elementary and middle schools. These schools are not necessarily affiliated with parishes. Different governance models, including governance by a board directly under the jurisdiction of the bishop, may be employed. The question of the regional school as a juridic person or part of a juridic person must be resolved under the direction of the bishop.

A fourth type of school is one operated by a religious congregation or other independent body, such as a board of trustees. Religious congregations and trustees are not generally as directly related to dioceses, as are the members of governing structures of other schools. The independent school may be a juridic person in its own right or it may be part of the juridic person represented by a religious congregation in the diocese.

The independent school owned by a Board of Trustees is much more common today than it was in 1991 when the first edition of this text appeared. In one scenario, a religious congregation owned the school and decided, usually in the face of limited finances and dwindling vocations, to withdraw overall financial support from the school. Congregations may have sold the school to a board of trustees with the provision that the property would revert to the religious congregation if the school closed. As with the other types of schools discussed above, these schools are subject to the bishop's authority in matters of faith and morals. Independent Catholic schools and their board members must understand and accept the bishop's authority in these matters; to attempt to act in a manner contrary to the wishes of the bishop could place a school's continuation as a Catholic school at risk.

There are also some independent schools that have dropped the word "Catholic" from their official titles. Literature may identify such a school as, e.g., "Sts. Augustine and Monica School, an independent school in the Catholic tradition." It is important for the boards of such schools to understand that one cannot be both truly Catholic and completely independent. The ability of those governing a school to call it a "Catholic" school requires that the authority of the bishop, as outlined in canon law, be recognized. Before a decision to drop "Catholic" from a school's name is made, the ramifications of such a step should be seriously examined. There is no evidence to indicate that a civil court would allow a school to call itself "Catholic" in defiance of the diocesan bishop's directive.

Catholic School Boards and the Law

Readers are directed to the NCEA publication by this author, *A Primer on Law for Administrators, Board Members,* etc., for a thorough analysis of Catholic school boards and the legal issues impacting them. A brief discussion follows.

Catholic school boards have important responsibilities. It is crucial that board members understand that whatever power a board has is vested in the board as a body, not in individual members. Board members must understand what the role of the board is – the development and/or recommendation of policy.

With the exception of high school boards and some regional school boards, the movement in the United States is towards advisory boards, rather than boards with specific jurisdiction. Advisory boards are consultative. Their function is to give advice and offer consultation as requested; it is not to "govern" the school. The actions of an advisory/consultative board are subject to the decision of the pastor who has the authority to accept or decline the recommendations of the consultative board.

A board with limited jurisdiction is one that has been *"constituted... to govern the parish education program, subject to certain decisions which are reserved to the pastor and the bishop"* (CACE/NABE, p. 27). This type of board would have, in both theory and practice, more autonomy in decision-making than would the consultative board because decision making powers have been delegated to the board.

A thorough discussion of types of boards can be found in *A Primer on Education Governance in the Catholic Church,* published by the Chief Administrators of Catholic Education, National Association of Boards of Education of the NCEA.

Whether a board is advisory or has limited jurisdiction, its role is defined by policy. Policy is usually defined as a guide for discretionary action. Policy will determine *what* the board wishes to be done. Policy is not concerned with administration or implementation; i.e., the board should not become involved in *how* its directives will be implemented or with *who are* the specific persons to implement them. For example, a board might adopt or recommend a policy requiring all teachers employed by the school to hold state certification. The board should not be concerned with *which* teachers a principal decides to hire. Such questions are administrative ones; they are to be determined by the principal or other chief executive officer of the school. Administrative decisions are the day-to-day management choices of the principal. It is crucial that everyone understand these realities from the outset.

When tensions arise, as they almost inevitably do, board members must keep their responsibilities to the diocese and to the church in view. Board members must be able to support the policies that are adopted, but support does not necessarily mean agreement. Support does mean a willingness to live with and not criticize the decision. If a person cannot support the policy, then change must be sought through the appropriate channels. If change cannot be achieved and the board member still cannot support the policy in question, then the person's only real choice is to resign from the board. The board member has to remember that the board's responsibilities are really two-fold: (1) to develop policies; and, (2) to support the persons and activities that implement those policies.

Disagreements should remain in the boardroom. Board members must remember that, as individuals, they have no real power. The power is vested in the board sitting as a body.

Becoming involved in internal, administrative school conflicts only weakens the authority of both the board and the administrator. Board members have a right, however, to expect that the principal or other administrator will keep them informed about problematic situations so that they will be able to respond intelligently, if questioned.

As stated above, canon law governs the Catholic school. Thus Catholic schools and board members have no authority to act outside the provisions of canon law. But within those provisions, boards have great freedom so long as no civil laws are broken.

Keeping Legally Sound Minutes

Education board members and principals often ask questions about the keeping of minutes: *"How do we best keep minutes? What should be in the minutes? Who should have access?"*

Many theories abound. Some persons advise recording everything that transpires in a meeting. Others advise writing as little as possible. Others suggest a compromise between the two positions. One reality, however, is ever-present. What is written becomes a legal record and can be used both for and against the institution. Developing a planned, orderly, consistent approach to taking and keeping minutes is imperative.

Does State Law Govern Catholic Education Board Meetings?

Catholic education boards govern private, not-for-profit, 501(c)3 organizations; as such, they are not generally subject to the same regulations as public organizations. Therefore, in the majority of cases, so-called "sunshine laws" requiring that meetings and the records of meetings be open to public scrutiny will not apply.

What Are Minutes?

Minutes are the written, legal record of actions taken at an official meeting of an official body. *Robert's Rules of Order*, the bible for meeting process, states that the following should be included in minutes:

(1) the name of the organization (school board, parish council, parents' organization, etc.),

(2) the date of the meeting,

(3) the place of the meeting (particularly if the meeting is held at a place other than the customary meeting place),

(4) presence of the regular presiding officer (president, principal, chair, etc.) and recording secretary or their substitutes,

(5) names of members, present and absent,

(6) approval of the minutes of the last scheduled meeting of the board (If the minutes are corrected, the corrections should be made in writing on the written minutes presented to the body for approval; new, corrected minutes should not be generated),

(7) officers and committee reports (the fact that a report was given is generally sufficient; the report can also be included as an attachment to the minutes),

(8) all motions, including

   (a) the name of the person who made the motion,

   (b) the fact that the motion was seconded (the name of the person seconding the motion is not absolutely required),

   (c) the complete text of the motion,

(9) the vote on the motion

   (a) number of votes for and against and

   (b) if a roll call vote is taken, the names of those voting for and against are documented,

(10) any appeals or points of order taken (not an ordinary occurrence),

   and,

(11) beginning and ending times of the meeting.

How Detailed Should the Minutes Be?

Conventional wisdom suggests that less, rather than more, is the acceptable norm. This author has consulted a number of attorney colleagues practicing in the not-for-profit arena. To a person, the advice given was: *"Say as little as possible. Accurately record actions taken. Do not document discussion or who said what. Anything you write can be used against you in a court of law, especially when taken out of context."*

How Should Executive Session Meetings Be Documented?

An executive session occurs when the board determines that it will meet with only the members and guests invited for a specific reason, such as attorneys, in a confidential session. A wise course of action is only to record actions taken (motions passed). Much confidential information is often shared in executive sessions, such as personnel and financial information. The information and the discussion surrounding it should not be recorded in the minutes. Additionally, if legal counsel is present at an executive session, the attorney/client privilege may be lost if legal advice and discussion are recorded in the minutes.

Who Should Have Access to Minutes?

To a great extent, the answer to this question should be determined at the local level. Many parishes routinely publish the minutes of the parish council, for example, in the parish bulletin. Some schools post the minutes of their board meetings on the school's web site.

Members of the board receive copies of the minutes. Policy should determine who else has access. A board might keep separate records of executive session meetings and not allow access to those records to anyone other than board members.

Some Do's and Don'ts For Keeping Minutes

(1) Do record only what must be recorded.

(2) Do not document discussion. Do record the names of those making motions or, if a roll call vote is

taken, who voted for and against a particular motion.

(3) Do follow the rule: *"Whatever is written should be specific, behaviorally oriented and verifiable."* For Example: Mr. Jones made the following motion: *"The salary for beginning teachers with no experience will be $24,000 for the '04-'05 school year."* After being seconded, the motion passed unanimously.

(4) Do enact a policy governing access to minutes.

(5) Keep an accurate, complete set of official minutes in a safe, secure place.

Protecting Board Members:
Liability and Insurance Questions

Persons serving on school boards often have questions concerning their personal civil liability if an individual should sue the school board. Historically, the doctrine of charitable immunity protected Catholic schools and those persons associated with them; this doctrine has been generally abandoned. However, many states have passed laws that specifically protect members serving on boards of non-profit organizations, such as religiously-affiliated schools, from civil liability. These laws presume *good faith* on the part of the board member; i.e., a person is expected to act in the best interests of those served. Good faith is a traditional defense to most claims against board members in both the public and private sectors. Nonetheless, schools and dioceses, as a matter of justice, should obtain and fund liability insurance for board members

The best protection from a lawsuit is the effort to act always in accord with justice. The school should provide some in-service education in the legal aspects of board membership. The diocesan attorney will be able to provide information concerning the laws of a given state and appropriate advice when questions concerning legal aspects arise.

The Principal's Rights & Responsibilities

The principal has the right and responsibility to administer the school. No one should interfere with that prerogative without serious cause. The principal is entitled to the support of the bishop, the superintendent, the pastor, and the school board. If, for sufficient reason, any one or more of those parties cannot support the principal and an acceptable compromise cannot be reached, the principal may have to leave the situation. Reasonable, good people can differ on how things should be done and a "parting of the ways" does not necessarily mean that one party is right and the other party is wrong. In any case, all parties have the obligation to support one another publicly and to address differences only in the appropriate forum.

Principals have numerous responsibilities, many of which are not found enumerated in any document. The safest course of action for principals is probably to assume that they are responsible for everything in their schools, unless responsibility for some aspect is clearly held by someone else. Much like the bishop and the pastor, the principal may delegate decision-making powers to other persons, but the responsibility cannot be delegated. If a lawsuit is brought against a school, it is extremely likely that the principal will be named as well; if a teacher is used, under the previously mentioned doctrine of *respondeat superior*, the principal also will generally be named.

Principals have two main legal responsibilities: (1) policy development – which most likely will be subject to review by a board, pastor or other party – and implementation of rules and policies and, (2) supervision of teachers and other personnel. Virtually every activity a principal engages in can be placed under one of these two categories.

One of the principal's most serious responsibilities is the supervision and evaluation of teachers. It is crucial that everyone understand that supervision and evaluation of personnel are the principal's responsibilities. In reality, supervision is quality control for the school.

The principal is legally responsible for both instructional quality and student well-being; neither can be assessed without spending time in classrooms. Persons, problems, and situations facing administrators on a daily basis claim time and attention. It is far too easy to neglect supervision when one is confronted with numerous other administrative tasks. Many threats of lawsuits could be avoided if principals and other administrators simply followed existing policy. It is extremely unnerving for a teacher if the principal who scheduled a supervisory visit does not appear and, perhaps worse, makes no mention of having missed the visit. Everyone understands that emergencies can happen; but once normalcy returns, the administrator should return to the regular supervisory/evaluative cycle.

Supervision and evaluation of teachers are matters of personnel policy. The faculty handbook should clearly delineate policies and procedures so that every teacher knows what to expect.

Frequency & Format

Administrators have a responsibility to supervise and evaluate teachers. Teachers have the right to know how often they can expect to be supervised and what format the report of the supervisory visit will take. Supervision can be problematic for both the principal and the teacher. A principal who never taught any grade below sixth, for example, may feel inadequate in a primary teacher's classroom; a high school principal who taught English may feel less than competent in a physics classroom. However, administrators and all effective educators should be able to recognize good teaching. If a principal is clearly "out of" his or her league in a certain content area, the assistance of someone with subject area competency can be sought.

If supervision is an ongoing, *formative* process, then both principal and teacher can grow together and help each other to improve the learning environment of the school. If supervision is viewed as punitive, as something that is only engaged in if the principal is "out to get" the teacher, it will hardly be successful.

Evaluation is *summative*: an administrator sums up all the available data and makes a decision regarding contract renewal. Evaluation of teaching performance, then, should be based on more than supervisory data. A principal will seek to answer such questions as: Does this teacher support the rules of the school? Does he or she look after the safety of the children as well as: *"Is he or she a good subject matter teacher?"* Evaluation, then, is a broader concept than supervision, but both should be present in a good school.

All administrators must understand that teachers and administrators are in schools for the students; the students are not there for the adults' employment. Surely, there is no more sacred responsibility than ensuring that students are being taught by capable, competent, caring professionals and that all teachers are encouraged and given the means to become the best professionals they can be. Supervision and evaluation enable a principal to make sound decisions about contract renewal. It is not just for a principal to decline to renew a teacher's contract if the principal has never observed the teacher.

Written observations that have been shared with teachers provide some of the best data for making employment decisions. A principal can use the data to plan and set goals with teachers. The handbook should state the school policy concerning supervision of teachers. Who is responsible for supervising teachers? Is it the principal's sole responsibility, or are other persons, such as assistant principals, department heads, or others involved? How often will the teacher be supervised? What format will be used?

Scheduled *v.* Unscheduled Visits

Will the supervisor's visits be scheduled or unscheduled? If the visits are normally scheduled for twice a year, does the principal reserve the right to observe classes at unscheduled times? The teacher also has a right to know how evaluation will occur. How will the supervisory visit data be incorporated into the end-of-the-year evaluation? Who will see this evaluation? Will the evaluation become part of the teacher's permanent file? Does the teacher have an opportunity to respond in writing to the evaluation? Will the teacher's response become part of the evaluation record? Considering these questions and developing policies to answer them will help an administrator operate on solid legal ground.

Although most educators would agree that supervision is a formative experience and evaluation is a summative one, the distinction becomes blurred in many Catholic schools where one administrator serves as both supervisor and evaluator. Teachers may be reluctant to discuss problems with principals in supervisory situations if they suspect that the information could be later used against them in evaluation. Thus, the administrator who "wears both hats" must be especially sensitive to the distinct issues of each function.

Good practice and civil law demand that administrators supervise teachers. Teachers should welcome supervision, both as a means of professional development and as legal protection if teaching competency is ever questioned.

Dealing With the "Problem" Employee: Creating a Paper Trail

The faculty handbook and/or the employment contract should state, at least in general terms, the reasons for which a teacher may be terminated. The most important factor to keep in mind in any termination or non-renewal situation is documentation. The best protection against a successful lawsuit is a written record of the reasons and events leading to termination.

The principal should document all events that illustrate what it is that makes an employee ineffective or undesirable. Administrators should bear in mind that teachers may be doing an adequate job in the classroom, but may be behaving in ways that are unacceptable outside the classroom. Some examples might be excessive absenteeism, tardiness, lack of cooperation, etc. Documentation should describe behavior and avoid judgments. It would be better to record: *"In a three day period, Mr. Jones sent twenty students to the office for misbehaving,"* than to state, *"Mr. Jones is having difficulty keeping order."*

One frequently-asked question concerns how to document meetings with employees who are having job performance problems and who perhaps may not be offered contracts for the coming year. In extreme cases, a principal may be considering terminating a teacher's employment during the year if improvement is not forthcoming. The following is a checklist for meeting with such employees. It is similar to procedures used in many businesses. Following these steps can help to ensure that an appropriate documentation trail has been kept should administrative actions ever be challenged in court.

Points for Conferencing With Problem Employees

1. Enumerate precisely what is wrong and needs improvement.

2. State that the school wants the teacher to improve.

3. State what the school is going to do to help the teacher.

4. Give a deadline at which time all parties will review improvement or lack of it.

5. Tell the employee that, if there is no improvement within the time frame stated, disciplinary action will result.

6. Give the teacher a copy of the conference document stating the first five points and ask the teacher to comment on the document to ensure understanding.

7. Have the employee sign the document and add any comments he or she wishes to include; if the teacher refuses to sign, have another person present to witness the refusal.

CHAPTER FIVE

PARENTS, STUDENTS AND TEACHERS: RIGHTS AND RESPONSIBILITIES

The most basic right of parents and students in a Catholic school is the right to receive a Catholic education. While the statement may appear obvious, it is important for everyone to remember that schools exist for students. Students do not attend school to provide employment for principals and teachers. The primary purpose of schools should be the principle by which all actions are judged. Anything that interferes with the education of students should not be permitted, whether that interference originates with parents, teachers, students, or others.

Catholic school principals face the challenges of respecting student and parent rights while upholding discipline and order. Common law and common sense indicate that persons and institutions responsible for the education of young people are expected to hold students to appropriate standards of behavior. Chapters I and II have discussed the fact that the main source of the law governing Catholic schools is contract law. The chapters also offered some information concerning the rights of those in public schools. The wise Catholic school administrator will be familiar with both the differences and similarities between the laws impacting their schools and the public schools.

Student Rights

While Catholic schools are not required to provide Constitutional due process protections to students, administrators are required to exercise fairness in their interactions with students. At minimum, as stated elsewhere in this text, a person accused of an infraction will be (1) told of the charges; and (2) allowed to respond to them (3) before an impartial tribunal. The Gospel requires that parents and students be treated fairly in Catholic schools. Fairness should be a goal of any institution purporting to prepare students for life. Deprivation of rights without the at least the offer of an unbiased hearing before penalties are imposed is not fundamentally fair. The days of announcing: *"This class will stay after school and you all know why,"* are clearly over. Parents and students have the right to demand fair treatment.

Although contract law is generally held to apply in cases involving Catholic schools, courts historically have provided little protection to students on the basis of that law. That reality is beginning to change. As Catholic school administrators require parents to sign statements that they have read and agree to be governed by the handbook of the school, so will courts require the school and its administrators to keep their "end of the bargain."

In the 1990s, courts seemed to disregard the doctrine of *in loco parentis*, schools and teachers stand "in the place of parents," which had previously been used to justify almost any action teachers took that a parent might take. In more recent times, however, the doctrine appears to have taken on new life. A sort of companion doctrine, the fiduciary theory, which holds that persons must take at least as much care of that which is entrusted to them as they would take if the entrusted entity were their own, has also arisen. Following this theory means that teachers and principals are expected to take care of their students in the same way they would care for their own children.

Most school administrators and attorneys would agree that the best school law, is like medicine, preventive. The best defense to a lawsuit is having tried to follow the right course in the first place. Catholic educators must realize that despite their best efforts in any and all areas of school life, they may well face lawsuits. All administrators must look carefully at their rules and procedures to ensure that they are reasonable, fair, and consistent, or else face the possibility of incurring problems and the expense of being sued.

In 1978, E. Edmund Reutter, Jr., after an analysis of hundreds of public school cases, offered six minimum essentials for developing enforceable rules of conduct. These essentials, as relevant today as they were when written, are: (1) the rule must be published to students; (2) the rule must have a rational legitimate educational purpose; (3) the rule must have a rational relationship to the achievement of the stated educational purpose; (4) the meaning of the rule must be reasonably clear; (5) the rule must be sufficiently narrow in scope so as not to encompass Constitutionally protected activities along with those which may be proscribed in schools; and, (6) if the rule infringes upon a Constitutional right, the compelling interest of the school in the enforcement of the rule must be shown.

While the fifth and sixth rules do not apply to Catholic schools, the other four are certainly worthy of consideration when developing rules and regulations. The *Gorman* case discussed in Chapter Two does suggest that courts may give private institutions wide latitude in developing rules. The rule in question in *Gorman* involved a hair length requirement for male students. The Rhode Island Supreme Court basically held that a private school may have any rule it wishes so long as the rule does not violate public policy or, to borrow a somewhat dated phrase, "shock the conscience of the court." Administrators should remember that it is much easier to make and implement fair rules from the outset than to try to undo damage resulting from poorly constructed and/or unfairly implemented rules.

It is the responsibility of the principal, as defined in the last chapter, to develop rules, promulgate them, and supervise their implementation. A principal must be sure that students and parents know the rule and that staff is enforcing the rule. If through the negligence of staff or administration, students honestly do not know of a rule's existence, they can hardly be held accountable for following the rule. If teachers are responsible for the implementation of rules, it is important that principals supervise teachers in the implementation of rules as well as in the delivery of instruction.

Administrators should strive for consistent enforcement of rules, although as the case of *Flint v. St. Augustine High School* indicates, just because a rule has not been consistently enforced does not mean it can never be enforced.

Flint involved two young men expelled from a Catholic high school for a second violation of a no smoking rule. Although the handbook clearly provided for such disciplinary action, no one had actually been expelled for such an offense prior to the expulsion of the plaintiffs, although other students had been guilty of the same offense. The judges stated that while they regretted the school's decision, under the doctrine of judicial restraint, they had to respect the school's decision if it acted within the scope of its authority. The court stopped short of saying that a Catholic school could arbitrarily dismiss students at will when it stated: *"That is not to say that due process safeguards can be cavalierly ignored or disregarded. But, if there is color of due process that is enough"* (p. 234). Although the court ruled in the school's favor, the reader can easily see that consistency would have provided the school with a stronger defense; certainly, fairness would seem to require that all schools attempt to be consistent in their enforcement of disciplinary policies.

The importance courts rightfully place on the development, promulgation, and implementation of rules is significant. Since handbooks and other written agreements can be construed as part of the contract existing between the school and its students and their parents, it is important that, as far as possible and practical, rules be in writing.

Courts look for evidence of good faith: did the institution have a rule? Was that rule promulgated? Did students and parents know of the rule? The court does not concern itself with the wisdom of the rule or even with the rightness or wrongness of the professional opinion of educators. Courts appear to be concerned only with the existence of a properly promulgated rule and with evidence that the institution acted in good faith according to the procedures it stated would be followed. Courts expect basic fairness in the execution of the contract between parent and school when considering allegations that a school acted improperly in its imposition of disciplinary sanctions.

School officials should understand that they will never be able to list every possible infraction a student could commit. Therefore, it is advisable to have some type of "catch all" clauses such as *"other inappropriate conduct,"* or, *"conduct, whether inside or outside school, that is detrimental to the reputation of the school."* Parents and students need to understand that what a student does, even if it occurs on the student's "own" time, outside the school day and property, reflects on the school. Parents of students in Catholic schools as well as the students themselves should understand that they are members of a faith and educational community and they have a responsibility to conduct themselves appropriately.

Recommendations for Rule Development

All Catholic schools should develop clear rules governing student behavior and clear procedures for dealing with misbehavior. Catholic educators must be concerned with being models of moral, ethical behavior; disciplinary policies and procedures must be examined in the light of Gospel principles and of the fundamental dignity that is the right of all persons.

The beginning point for the development of rules should be the school's mission statement and philosophy. Principals must ensure that there is a clearly written mission statement that informs all the activities of the school. The mission statement and philosophy must be viewed as living documents, not as something that was written once and has been put away somewhere to be brought out when the occasion requires it. No teacher should be employed unless the teacher has read the mission statement and the philosophy and agreed to support them. Everyone in the school community should understand the mission statement and be able to articulate it. Even very young children can be brought to some understanding of the mission statement: *"At our school we try to treat each other the way Jesus would treat us."* The life of the school should be seen as flowing out of the mission statement.

If rules are clearly written, there is less likelihood that serious problems will arise when penalties are imposed. A rule stating: *"Students are not to be late for class"* could be considered vague; a rule stating: *"Students arriving after the bell rings will be marked late,"* is much clearer and less open to debate.

Whenever possible, rules should be written, a requirement supported by common sense reasons. It is easier to display the written rule when emotions run high than to insist that *"at the beginning of the school year, you were told about this rule."*

Every school should have a written parent/student handbook. Schools should consider having parents and older students sign a form, stating that they have read the rules and agree to be governed by them. A written handbook should encourage the school to strive for clarity in rule making. Periodic evaluation should enable the school to make necessary changes in rules. (Readers desiring more information about handbook development may wish to consult the NCEA publication, *School Handbooks* (2nd edition) by this author.)

When considering the development of disciplinary guidelines and procedures, educators must be aware that there is a time investment involved. If students are allowed to tell their side(s) of a story, the educator is committing to spending time with students. The benefit should be obvious: students perceive persons in authority as trying to be fair and will internalize the values that are modeled. If students see an educator behaving in a manner that is respectful of their dignity, they may be more likely to afford that same respect to others. This type of behavior will ensure that a school and its officials are acting in a fair manner and, in the case of litigation, will offer a sound defense. Catholic educators, then, should commit themselves to notice and a hearing in any disciplinary situation; in this way, the school acts in a fair and moral manner.

Somewhat more extensive procedures should be developed if the penalty is suspension. One-day suspensions should minimally require that the disciplinarian, or whoever administers discipline for the school, rather than an individual teacher, be involved and that parents be notified. Longer suspensions should involve written notification specifying the charges and stating the time and place of the disciplinary hearing. Cases in which the possibility of expulsion exists require written notification and a more formal hearing. Careful documentation should be kept in all disciplinary proceedings.

The right of the student to legal counsel in suspension and expulsion hearings is a controversial one. Catholic educators should understand that there is no legal requirement that a Catholic school permit legal counsel to be present at a disciplinary hearing; however, if the school grants that privilege to one student, it may be setting a precedent.

The presence of attorneys creates an adversarial atmosphere of necessity and may well lessen the possibility of Christian reconciliation. This author believes that Catholic schools should not allow the presence of attorneys at disciplinary hearings.

These recommendations may be helpful to Catholic school administrators as they attempt to develop, modify, and implement rules and policies. Ultimately, the guiding principle should be the desire to act in a reasonable, moral way consistent with the Gospel, one's philosophy, and the principles of canon law.

The Rights of Parents

As nearly every educator would agree, parents are the primary educators of their children. They are the ones who should know the most about the children. In the best of all situations, school and parents work together for the good of the child. (The small NCEA booklet, *Your Rights and Responsibilities in a Catholic School*, written for parents by this author may be helpful.)

Parents have the right to expect that: (1) their children will receive what they "are paying for," i.e., a Catholic education; (2) they will be able to present their concerns and discuss them in a respectful atmosphere; (3) they will receive timely responses to written requests and phone calls; (4) they will be encouraged to visit their children's classrooms; (5) they will be notified of their children's academic and behavioral progress or lack thereof; (6) their children will be treated fairly and, (7) they will be promptly informed of any changes in rules and regulations.

Sometimes, however, the partnership simply does not work. Occasionally, a principal may express the belief that nothing that is done will ever please a certain parent. A parent may demand an inordinate amount of a teacher's or administrator's time. A parent may refuse to accept the discipline meted out to his or her child. A parent may refuse to follow school rules. In such a situation, of course, every possible attempt should be made to reach a resolution that all can accept. In extreme cases, such a resolution may not be forthcoming and the school administrator may be forced to ask the parent to withdraw the child from school and if warranted, require the withdrawal. Some administrators are now including statements such as: *"The education of your child is a partnership between you and the school. If, in the opinion of school administrators, the partnership is irretrievably broken, you may be required to withdraw your child from the school."*

The majority of parents will, it is hoped, be supportive and helpful. In a community where all members are valued and each member fulfills his or her responsibility, a thriving faith and educational community will be found that will benefit all, especially the students.

The Rights & Responsibilities of Teachers

Just as the rights of students in Catholic schools are significantly different from those of public school students, so, too, do the rights of Catholic schoolteachers differ from those of their public school counterparts. Unless state action can be demonstrated, Catholic school personnel can claim no protected activities under the Constitution and no due process protections under the Fifth and Fourteenth Amendments. Nonetheless, Catholic schoolteachers do have rights. These are generally conferred by the contract or agreement existing between the school and the teacher and so, the law of contracts governs the employment situation. State and federal statutes confer other rights as well. Common law demands that persons treat other persons according to certain accepted standards of behavior.

Personnel Issues

The personnel issues confronting Catholic school administrators today are not the ones of the 1950s and 60s. Religious receiving small stipends no longer staff the vast majority of Catholic schools. Administrators must navigate the issues of paying appropriate salaries to teachers, providing employee benefits, and developing legally sound employment policies and procedures.

School officials must examine the legal soundness of actions and documents. Administrators should attempt to match their deeds with their words. Constraints, including financial ones, must be balanced against the requirements of justice. If an administrator moves outside the parameter of civil law, everything inside the parameter can be lost. Disagreements between Catholic school personnel and officials cannot always be solved in the pastor's parlor or the principal's office. Regrettably, some disagreements propel the participants into court.

Subsidiarity and collegiality are values that should inform relationships and structures within the church. Subsidiarity requires that persons having disagreements or complaints should seek discussion and resolution of the problem at the level closest to the problem. Therefore, the teacher who has a disagreement with the principal should not contact the pastor, board, superintendent, or bishop before an attempt is made to resolve the matter with the principal. If this process became standard practice in Catholic education, an untold number of problems might be solved before major crises develop, relationships rupture, and lawsuits are filed. Of course, such principles are generally easier in theory than in practice.

Courts generally uphold personnel actions in Catholic schools because of the First Amendment's protection of freedom of religion. As stated earlier, however, this protection is not absolute as was seen in the previously-discussed, 1982 case of *Reardon v. LeMoyne*, involving four women religious in conflict with the diocesan office.

On appeal, the state supreme court found that the doctrine of separation of church and state did not preclude jurisdiction in non-doctrinal contract matters:

> Religious entities, however, are not totally immune from responsibility under civil law. In religious controversies involving property or contractual rights outside the doctrinal realm, a court may accept jurisdiction and render a decision without violating the first amendment.... It is clear from the foregoing discussion that civil courts are permitted to consider the validity of non-doctrinal contractual claims which are raised by parties to contracts with religious entities. This requires the courts to evaluate the pertinent contractual provi-

sions and intrinsic evidence to determine whether any violations of the contract have occurred, and to order appropriate remedies, if necessary (pp. 431-32).

In essence, the state supreme court found that the trial court should have accepted jurisdiction over the bishop and the superintendent as well as over the school board members because the issue was a purely civil one. Furthermore, the court held that the trial court should have acted on the sisters' requests so that their rights would have been protected.

The *Reardon* court found that civil courts, while not allowed to interfere in purely doctrinal matters, did have jurisdiction over the civil employment contracts of church employees, including religious. The days of religious superiors' directing a religious to leave quietly and move on to a new assignment are largely over – as well they should be. Whatever rights are afforded lay personnel should also be given to religious. Conversely, whatever rules govern personnel should be applied equally to faculty members belonging to religious communities, the clergy, and the laity. There is no room for a privileged class or a double standard in Catholic schools.

Employment Policies

Dioceses, parishes, and schools are responsible for developing polices that protect the contractual rights of personnel. A school has a contract with its teachers, and the faculty handbook can be considered part of the contract. Contracts place certain obligations upon teachers, but they also place obligations upon the employer. It is important that the diocesan and parish school's policies be in line with those of the diocese, especially since most teacher contracts bind the teacher to observe the policies and regulations of the diocese. In a strictly legal sense, a non-diocesan Catholic school is not bound by every diocesan mandate for schools. However, since a school can call itself Catholic only with the approval of the bishop, it makes sense that Catholic schools would strive for *voluntary* compliance with diocesan policies whenever possible.

Dioceses are certainly free to develop guidelines in addition to, or in place of policies. Generally, a guideline allows more latitude on the part of the school than does a policy. However, dioceses should ensure that parishes, boards, pastors, and principals understand what is intended by the guideline: how binding is it? Are certain guidelines more binding than others? In some dioceses, there are no educational policies *per se* – there are only guidelines. Diocesan personnel should be in contact with the bishop who, in terms of canon law, is the only lawgiver, to be sure that diocesan handbooks reflect his wishes and that all relevant parties are made aware of the binding power of policies. (Readers may wish to consult the NCEA book by this author, *Policy Development in Catholic Schools*.)

Hiring policies are very important. Procedures must be in line with the requirements of civil law. Pre-employment inquiries carry the potential for violation of a person's rights. Administrators want to gather as much job-related information as possible, but at the same time invasion of privacy and discriminatory questions must be avoided.

Catholic school administrators have legitimate concerns about providing for stability on faculties and about ensuring that persons who are hired will have good attendance. Administrators may not, however, ask a woman if she intends to have children or whether baby-sitting will be a problem. Inquiries as to numbers of children and/or marital status are not permitted.

Job-related questions are allowed; some examples might be: *"Is there any condition or situation that may cause you to have a problem with regular attendance or performance of the job's duties?"* or, *"Are you a Catholic in good standing with the Church?"* Applicants can be asked about criminal records. As discussed in Chapter I, the mere fact that someone has been convicted of a crime does not mean that he or she must be automatically excluded from service in a Catholic school. A fifty-year-old man who served a year in jail for felony possession of marijuana at age eighteen, but who has had a spotless record since should not be excluded from consideration for employment solely on the basis of something that occurred thirty-two years ago. Convictions of sexual offenses, no matter how long ago, should always preclude an individual's being employed in a Catholic school.

Applicants should be asked to give written permission for background checks. The majority of states now require all persons who work in schools to be fingerprinted and/or to have a criminal records check.

Catholic Schools and Discrimination

Federal anti-discrimination law binds Catholic schools. Catholic schools are required to file statements of compliance with anti-discrimination laws with appropriate local, state and national authorities. Catholic schools, like all employers, are prohibited from discriminating on the basis of sex, race, color, national origin, age, and disability, if with reasonable accommodation, the needs of the otherwise qualified disabled person could be met. Catholic schools can discriminate on the basis of religion, and Catholic applicants can be given preference in hiring. Catholic school administrators must exercise caution and avoid even the slightest suggestion of inappropriate discrimination.

The case of *Dolter v. Wahlert* illustrates this. Ms. Dolter, an unmarried teacher in a Catholic high school, became pregnant. The principal later rescinded her contract, although evidence indicated that he was aware that male faculty members had also engaged in pre-marital sex, but had not disciplined them in any way. The court rejected a "separation of church and state" defense and ruled that the issue in this case was not premarital sex but sexual discrimination. In a somewhat humorous footnote to the case, the court stated: *"The court certainly can take judicial notice of the fact that under the present physiological laws of nature women are the only members of the human population who can become pregnant"* (p. 270). Anti-discrimination legislation can impact Catholics schools because the government has a compelling interest in the equal treatment of all citizens. Compliance with statutory law will be required if there is no less burdensome way to meet the requirements of the law. In *Dolter*, the court was careful to state that the non-renewal of the teacher's contract would have been upheld if men known to engage in premarital sex had been treated in the same manner. The problem was not the school's prohibition of premarital sex, but the unequal application of the prohibition on the basis of sex.

Age discrimination laws prohibit discrimination against persons over the age of 40. It is not permissible to ask a potential employee his or her age prior to employment. The only permissible question is: *"Are you over the age of 18?"* It is not uncommon to find Catholic school administrators who say: *"I prefer to hire a person right out of college or with little teaching experience. That way we don't have to pay a high salary."* True financial exigency can be a reason for choosing a less experienced, generally younger applicant. If an applicant over the age of forty were to challenge the hiring of a younger person, the school would not be in a very strong position to assert financial exigency, if non-essential expenses were paid. For example, a principal who declined to hire a teacher based on "no money to pay" and who subsequently made major, arguably unnecessary, purchases might be liable for age discrimination.

The existence of a disability in an applicant can be problematic for Catholic schools. As indicated above, Section 504 of the Rehabilitation Act of 1973 (as amended in 1974) can apply to schools receiving any sort of federal financial assistance. It has been argued that these types of assistance are not legally significant; however, few Catholic schools would want to be part of a test case. The Americans with Disabilities Act does have an exclusion for religious institutions, but this author believes it would be most unwise to rely on that exclusion. State laws can be even more restrictive than the ADA and can apply to all employers.

In brief, an applicant cannot be denied employment simply because he or she has a disability, if the applicant is otherwise qualified and can perform the essential functions of the job with reasonable accommodation. If the existence of a disability makes it impossible for an applicant to possess the bona fide occupational qualifications (BFOQs) for the job, employment can be denied on the basis of the applicant's not being qualified, rather than on the applicant's being disabled. For example, no one would hire a blind airline pilot because sight is a bona fide occupational qualification for flying an airplane. A blind individual denied employment as a pilot would not be experiencing discrimination; he or she simply would be considered "unqualified."

How Catholic Do Teachers Have To Be?

Today's Catholic educators talk a great deal about Catholic identity. What makes a school Catholic? How can a school and its staff claim its Catholic heritage? Does a teacher have to agree with everything the Church says? What should a teacher say if a student asks for her opinion and she doesn't agree with the Church's position? Isn't it dishonest to support a position one thinks is wrong? These are all questions that most readers will have heard. This author would posit that a Catholic school's first legal obligation is to be true to the teachings of the Catholic Church. No one is more important than faculty members in ensuring the Catholicity of the school.

What Makes a School Catholic?

Simply calling an institution Catholic does not make it so. Being Catholic requires a commitment to the Gospel, the teachings of Jesus Christ, and the teachings of the Roman Catholic Church, both when it is convenient to be committed and when it is not so convenient. If any of the above are compromised, the school is eroding its Catholicity, but one can legitimately argue that being Catholic is an either/or proposition: either the school is Catholic or it is not.

"Cafeteria" Approaches to Catholicism Not Permitted

In the 1970s, many in the church talked about a cafeteria approach to Catholicism: *"I like the church's teachings on social justice, so I'll support them. I think the church is wrong about birth control, so I'll follow my conscience – after all, doesn't the church teach that conscience is primary?"* These statements are probably familiar to many readers.

However, there is one basic bottom line. A Catholic educator's first legal duty is to be true to the teachings of the Catholic Church. A Catholic educator is an agent of the Catholic Church and has to hold the "company line," as this author often states. The situation is similar to that of any person who works for any organization. If an individual works for a company that makes umbrellas, he is expected to uphold the company's products. He probably will not be employed very long if he encourages people to buy plastic rain hoods as an alternative to umbrellas. Perhaps the analogy seems a bit simplistic, but the underlying premise is not: if one cannot support the company that one works for and the products the company produces, the honest course of action is to find another job. The product being sold is Catholic education. Parents send their children to Catholic schools for Catholic education, not for the private opinions of teachers, and they have a legal right to expect fidelity to Church teaching.

Isn't Conscience Primary?

The Catholic Church does teach that one's conscience, properly formed, is primary. But the question of agency is still the "sticking point." If one teaches in a Catholic school and is asked about a matter concerning which she has a different personal position than the one the church takes, she is not at liberty simply to share that opinion with the students in her classes because she is an agent of the Church, the same way a bishop or the pope is an agent.

A recent decision illustrates this. In the 2004 case, *Michele Curay-Cramer v. the Ursuline Academy of Wilmington, Delaware et al.*, a teacher signed an ad supporting a woman's right to choose to have an abortion. When school officials asked her to recant, she declined to do so. The school then terminated her employment. She brought suit alleging: gender discrimination, defamation, invasion of privacy, and tortuous interference with contractual relations. The judge, referring to the previously cited *NLRB v. the Catholic Bishop of Chicago* case, stated that the issue was whether Congress intended federal law, i.e., Title VII, which proscribes discrimination, to apply to such cases. In dismissing the case, the judge ruled that such an application would violate the free exercise rights of the Catholic Church and, additionally, would constitute an impermissible entanglement of church and state.

So What's an Educator to Do?

The Catholic educator must present the teachings of the Catholic Church. It is certainly permissible to say that some persons do not agree with whatever the teaching is, but one must be clear about what the church's position is. The educator is not free to say, for example: *"I think the Church is wrong about birth control. Responsible persons use artificial contraception,"* or, *"Women should be ordained. The Pope is wrong."* If pressed for a personal opinion, one can say: *"My personal opinion is not what we are discussing. The Church teaches...."*

Sometimes, this reality is painful. The Church does not claim to be perfect, but persons who are responsible for the Catholic education of young persons must teach them the precepts of the Church as the Church has taught them, not as individual teachers might like them to be. To do less is to fail in one's primary legal obligation.

Personal Conduct

Administrators are often faced with the issues of actual or perceived inappropriate staff conduct and may wonder what legal rights they have to demand certain standards of behavior from teachers, particularly during off-campus times. What a staff member does, both in and outside the educational setting, impacts the quality and integrity of ministry within the setting. The doctrine of separation of church and state protects principals and other administrators and allows them to set standards of personal behavior that would not be permitted in the public sector.

Behavioral Expectations for Catholic Educators

Contracts and other documents governing employment should state that staff members are expected to support the teachings of the Catholic Church through their behavior. Schools may have non-Catholic staff members and one would not expect such individuals to attend Mass outside the school on a regular basis or to be participating members of a parish. But non-Catholics who seek to acquire or retain positions in Catholic settings should expect that standards of behavior would be in force. For example, if the fact that an individual had an abortion becomes known and is a source of scandal, the school and/or parish has every right to terminate that individual's employment or volunteer status. To do otherwise might send a confusing message to parents, students, and the larger community.

Issues of Sexual Preference and/or Lifestyle

Issues of sexual preference pose special problems. While no one should condemn a homosexual orientation, a Catholic educational administrator as an agent of the Church, cannot ignore manifestations of an openly gay lifestyle that pose scandal.

Equally difficult decisions must be made in situations involving divorced staff members who remarry without an annulment if that fact becomes known. Even if the teacher in question is convinced that he or she is acting in good conscience in contracting a second marriage, there is little doubt that the person is, objectively speaking, in violation of church law and hence, a possible source of scandal. The situation is not a problem from the standpoint of terminating the employment of a person who violates church law. The school clearly can terminate the employment of one who violates religious norms. The problem is the lack of consistency from diocese to diocese, from school to school, and sometimes even within the same school. All persons and institutions are expected to be fair. How can an employer claim to be fair in dealings with employees if one employee is treated one way and a second employee another way for the same behavior, depending on who is involved? It is difficult to defend dismissal decisions on religious grounds if one person is dismissed for an action and another, having acted in the same manner, is retained. These principles hold in any case in which religious issues are involved. There is no easy solution, but governing boards and administrators have an obligation to see that the teachings of the Catholic Church are respected and not compromised in the witness given by staff members. Many dioceses have policies that are concerned with scandalous public behavior.

In summary, then, once an individual performs an act that is inconsistent with Church teaching and becomes publicly known, that person may no longer be qualified to work in a Catholic school at that time. While such a reality may seem obvious, it is recommended that documents state the requirement of supporting the teachings of the Church.

Illegal Activity

A person who has committed an illegal act may certainly have employment or volunteer status terminated. One who is convicted of, or who admits commission of, a crime should be removed from professional and/or volunteer status. The harder question arises when a person is simply accused of, or arrested on suspicion of, a crime. School officials may be sharply divided as to the proper response to make in such a situation.

The United States has long operated under the principle of "innocent until proven guilty." It may appear that, until guilt is established, the fair approach would be to let the person continue in his or her position. Yet, the reality often is that effectiveness in such situations is severely compromised.

How, then, should one deal with an arrest of, or serious accusation concerning, a teacher or other staff member? Every school should have a policy in place that allows the administrator to place the accused individual on a leave of absence pending the outcome of an investigation or an adjudication of guilt. The time to enact a policy is *not* when it is needed. The prudent administrator and educational board will have policy in place that anticipates such situations. While realizing the complexity inherent in these situations, administrators must ensure that fidelity to the Church and compliance with law characterize policies and procedures; the teacher or staff member must support the teachings of the Catholic Church.

It seems that the safest legal course for schools and dioceses to follow is to develop policy and to enforce it. As difficult as it may be to dismiss employees, it is unfair to pick and choose those who will be held to a policy. Justice demands that administrators construct policy that is applied equally to all.

Breach of Contract

Several breach of contract cases have been discussed earlier in the text. Principals and other administrators need to understand that courts construe contracts against the persons who wrote them; if there is any ambiguity in the contract provisions, the benefit of the doubt will go to the party who did not write the contract.

Either party to the contract – the school or the teacher, can commit breach of contract. It is generally conceded, however, that it is futile for a Catholic school to bring breach of contract charges against a teacher who wants to terminate a contract; to compel a person to teach against his or her will would be tantamount to involuntary servitude or slavery. Courts have ruled that since replacements are readily available, a school sustains no injury when a teacher leaves; without an injury, there can be no lawsuit. As frustrating as this reality can be for principals, it is simply a fact of life in the Catholic school.

Some persons suggest including liquidated or stipulated damages clauses in teacher contracts, i.e., a teacher who breaches a contract must pay a fee toward the cost of finding a replacement. The labor laws of most states do not permit withholding monies from salaries, so that a school could be forced to pursue a small claims action which could result in minimal payments, if any. In a 2004 Louisiana case, *Keiser v. Catholic Diocese of Shreveport, Inc.*, the Louisiana Appellate Court, 2nd Circuit, ruled that a stipulated damages clause in the contract which required the teacher to pay a certain amount of damages to the school if she left her position before the contract's end could not be enforced because: (1) it did not reflect the actual measure of damages; and, (2) it had never been enforced against any other employee. In fact, at the time of hiring, the teacher expressed concern about the clause and was informed by the principal that no one had ever been made to pay the money. Catholic school administrators would be well advised to forego liquidated or stipulated damages clauses in their employment contracts.

Schools are responsible for developing policies that protect the contractual rights of personnel. As stated previously, a court can consider the faculty or employee handbook to be part of the contract between the employee and the school. Contracts place certain obligations upon employees, but they also place obligations upon the employer. It is important that the school's policies be in line with those of the diocese, especially in view of the fact that most teacher contracts bind the teacher to follow the policies and regulations of the diocese and/or other sponsoring organization.

Discipline and Dismissal

Most cases involving teachers in both the public and private sectors are concerned with teacher dismissals and/or non-renewal of contracts. Obviously, a decision to dismiss or not to renew the contract of a teacher is one that an administrator should not make lightly and it is one that should be made only after other attempts at discipline of the faculty member have been made.

Although the Constitutional protections afforded public schoolteachers are not granted Catholic schoolteachers, contract law protects both sets of teachers. Administrators must honor the provisions of the contract or be able to give a legitimate reason for not doing so. Courts will scrutinize contracts to ensure that their provisions have been followed. While a Catholic school contract may be far less involved than a public school contract, it is nonetheless a contract.

Catholic school administrators should familiarize themselves with the laws governing dismissal of public school teachers in their states. The "lawful" reasons for dismissal of public school teachers are also reasons for dismissing Catholic schoolteachers. The following are generally considered to be grounds for dismissal.

Incompetency is a term that can encompass any of several conditions: physical or mental incapacity which is permanent and incurable, although federal laws prohibiting discrimination must be observed; lack of knowledge about the subject matter one is assigned to teach or lack of ability to impart that knowledge; failure to adapt to new teaching methods; physical mistreatment of students; violation of school rules; lack of cooperation; negligent conduct; failure to maintain discipline; and personal misconduct in or out of school that affects teaching performance. It is readily apparent that incompetency can encompass a wide range of behaviors.

Insubordination is generally the willful refusal to abide by the rules or directives of superiors. It can be distinguished from incompetency in that an incompetent person may be involved in the same behavior as an insubordinate employee, but the incompetent person is not assumed to be willfully violating duties and rules.

Unprofessional conduct is also a broad concept. It may be the same behavior as personal misconduct. However, while all personal misconduct can probably be construed as unprofessional conduct, not all unprofessional conduct is personal misconduct. For example, it might be considered unprofessional conduct to discuss confidential school matters at the dinner table; it would be difficult, however, to put that behavior in the same category as personal misconduct, such as sexual offenses or driving while intoxicated.

Immorality is listed in the statutes of many states as grounds for dismissal. Different communities have different standards of morality and those standards change with time. In addition, what is considered immoral and/or shocking in one part of the country may not be in another. Case law indicates that courts differ in their interpretation of what constitutes immorality and what constitutes unfitness to teach. In the public sector, at least, some courts have held that performing an immoral act (with the exception of sexual misconduct) may not be justification for terminating a teacher's employment unless it can be demonstrated that the immoral act or public knowledge of the immoral act impairs one's ability to be an effective teacher.

The Catholic school and its officials have a well-defined body of Church law to guide them in determining what is moral and what is not. Nonetheless, interpretations among reasonable people can differ considerably. Thus, it is extremely important that appropriate officials anticipate problem areas and plan policy accordingly. Just as a principal cannot foresee every possible action a student might take that could warrant expulsion, officials will not be able to compile a list of every immoral action applicable to every situation that may present itself. Discussion and planning before a problem appears can help to ease the difficulties that are always inherent in cases in which teachers are alleged to have acted in an immoral manner.

"Catch all" clauses such as "any other just reason" can be found in many state statutes. These clauses allow for action in situations that may not seem to be covered under any rule. For example, if a teacher were found innocent by reason of insanity of a serious crime, a school could possibly dismiss the teacher even in the absence of a pertinent statute or policy, because teaching effectiveness would certainly be impacted and, one could argue, the individual no longer possesses the bona fide occupational qualifications for the job.

Courts will generally apply the "whole record test" in teacher dismissal cases except in situations involving criminal conviction or gross misconduct. If an administrator is seeking to dismiss a teacher for incompetence, the dismissal will probably not be upheld if it is based on a single incident. The court will consider the whole record of the teacher in determining whether the dismissal was proper.

Policies governing non-renewal of contract and dismissal from employment should be in place in all Catholic schools. Non-renewal of contact and dismissal from employment are not synonymous terms. Non-renewal of contract does not carry the same connotation and stigma that dismissal from employment or "being fired" does. Sometime, the terms are used synonymously, although they should not be. Indeed, the way many contracts are written throughout the United States, Catholic schoolteachers may face non-renewal of contract every year because the contract contains a clause such as: *"This contract expires June 30 unless definitively renewed."* In many of these situations, there is little practical difference between non-renewal of contract. There is, however, a "world" of legal difference. A contract should identify the difference between non-renewal of contract at the end of a school year and termination during a school year, but it would be advisable to seek legal counsel in constructing such a document. Regardless of what one can do, one should obviously take great care in choosing not to renew the contract of a long time employee.

Tenure

Tenure considerations, while very different in the public and private sectors, are important in teacher dismissal. Almost every public institution has some provision for granting teacher tenure. While tenure is commonly considered to mean that a teacher has an expectancy of continued employment, it is important to remember that expectancy is not an absolute guarantee. Tenure is job protection. It is an assurance that if a teacher performs duties in a reasonable manner, the teacher can expect to be re-employed. Tenure is granted in the public school after a probationary period. State statutes may specify a given period of probation.

In most dioceses tenure does not exist. One exception would be those dioceses that have unions. A 1979 United States Supreme Court decision, *NLRB v. the Catholic Bishop of Chicago*, held that Catholic schools did not have to allow union representation or recognize unions. Unions that were in place in Catholic schools prior to this ruling were not affected by it, as courts and legislatures generally do not make retroactive laws. Private sector employment is said to be "at will." Employers generally hire and fire whom they please. As indicated in Chapter I though, there is some erosion of this doctrine. Employers are not allowed to terminate employees for "bad" reasons, reasons that violate public policy.

Although no court has yet held that Catholic schools can be compelled to reinstate wrongfully terminated teachers, courts have, as indicated above, ordered Catholic schools to pay damages to teachers who have successfully argued that their contracts had been breached.

The Importance of Following Policies

Teachers and other employees have a right to expect that the school's policies will be followed fairly and applied equally to all employees. Problems can arise when conflicting policies exist. In the *Reardon* case, part of the problem was the conflicting policy statements regarding the continuation of employment. The difficulties of inconsistency are obvious; administrators need to ensure that documents are consistent.

In keeping with fairness and due process considerations, dioceses and schools should develop policies requiring that a teacher facing suspension or dismissal be told of the charges and be given an opportunity to refute them. Some process for appeal should be in place. In many dioceses, the bishop is the last "court of appeal." It is important that there be some avenue of appeal for employees, particularly ones who have served in a particular school for many years.

Civil law provides many "do's and don'ts" for those responsible for the operation of Catholic schools. It is necessary, however, to remember that civil law is only one parameter surrounding and providing rules for the ministry of Catholic education. The Gospel and the example of Jesus' life surely provide another. In dealing with students, parents, teachers, and others, the administrator should always consider the demands of both parameters before determining a course of action.

CHAPTER SIX

SPECIAL TOPICS

In the preceding five chapters, the author has attempted to offer an overview of civil law affecting Catholic schools and an analysis of the specifics of laws as they apply to those schools, as well as to those who: govern them, attend them, trust their children to them, and minister within them. This chapter will discuss in some depth topics that were not included, or included only peripherally, in the first edition of this text.

Boundaries

The topic of boundaries in professional relationships has remained in the forefront of discussions on Catholic education for some time. Today, everyone seems to be talking about boundaries, the keeping of them, the prevention of boundary violation, and the avoidance of litigation prompted by the appearance of impropriety. The tragedy of the sexual abuse crisis has forced many to reflect on how they relate to those they serve – and that reflection is a good and necessary action. It is too easy to forget that teachers, administrators, and other staff members are professionals rendering a service. Just as a counselor or psychiatrist is professionally bound to avoid emotional involvement with a client, an educator should strive to avoid becoming so emotionally involved with a student that objectivity and fairness are compromised. Teachers and other staff members must remember that they have many persons for whom they are responsible and who need and may desire their attention. If a relationship with one student keeps a teacher from responding to other needs on a regular basis, the teacher should examine the appropriateness of the relationship seriously. Administrators, who become aware of such situations, have an absolute responsibility to bring them to the attention of the teachers involved and help them "think through the situation" and decide on appropriate behavior.

What is the Responsibility of an Administrator Who Only Has a Suspicion?

Administrators must trust themselves and their intuition. If something doesn't feel right or causes discomfort, there is probably cause for concern. This author believes that one reason such situations escalate into serious, even tragic, outcomes is because those in authority are fearful of saying anything without proof. As in most other ministerial situations, approach is everything. If an administrator notices a teacher and a student, in each other's company fairly constantly and others are beginning to talk, the administrator does not have to confront the teacher with an allegation of sexual misconduct. Rather, the administrator could gently point out that he or she has become aware of some talk that involves the two and that the administrator wants to make the teacher aware of the talk. The administrator could then discuss the reality of perception. The leadership guru, Tom Peters, is often quoted as saying: *"Perception is all there is."* In essence, what people think they see is what they consider fact. All administrators would do well to reflect on this statement, not just for problematic situations, but also to determine personal behavior that might be perceived differently than it is intended.

Relationships with Persons Under the Age of 18

Another behavioral concern deals with the legal risks posed by student/staff relationships. Obviously, adults want to demonstrate personal interest in young people. It is a sad reality, however, that administrators must be vigilant in monitoring staff behavior in an effort to avoid even the appearance of impropriety.

Staff members care about students. That care may extend to all areas of life. Teachers often find themselves counseling students in personal matters. It is not unusual for a teacher or other staff member to find him/herself in the position of "surrogate parent." Young people often entrust both professional and non-professional staff with confidential information. Staff members, many with little training in professional counseling, often question what is appropriate in interacting with young people.

Few guidelines are available. Teachers and other personnel often deal with situations that pose both personal and legal risks for the adults as well as for the students. This author is familiar with several situations in which parents threatened and/or pursued legal action against a teacher whose actions they viewed as unwise, inappropriate, sexually motivated, or interfering with the parent/child relationship. All adults working in the educational ministry of the church should be aware of the legal ramifications involved in student/staff relationships and be careful to avoid the perception as well as the reality of inappropriateness.

Sexual Misconduct

Allegations of sexual misconduct can be devastating. Sexual misconduct *can* be alleged in apparently innocent situations. Young persons *can* misinterpret touching and a staff member could find him/herself facing child abuse charges. Extreme caution is in order whenever an adult touches a minor.

A minor who believes that an adult has not responded to efforts to achieve a closer relationship poses another kind of problem. Such a student may accuse a teacher of inappropriate conduct as a retaliatory measure. Educators must be aware that serious consequences can result from an allegation of child abuse, even if that allegation is eventually proven to be false. At the very least, such a false allegation can be extremely embarrassing for the educator. If a child abuse report is made, authorities will question the adult and the investigation will be recorded. States retain lists of suspected child abusers.

Fear of teachers facing child abuse allegations has caused some public school districts in this country to adopt rules that prohibit any faculty touching of students. Such rules preclude putting one's arm around students, patting a student on the back, and giving a student a hug. No Catholic educator would probably want to take such a position, but common sense precautions must be taken for the protection of all.

Avoiding the Appearance of Impropriety: Recommendations for Keeping Boundaries

In response to many requests to develop a "don'ts" list on the topic of boundaries for educators, the writer has prepared the following. Each "don't" is followed by a brief commentary.

1. **Do not stay alone in a room with a student unless there is a window permitting others to see in or the door is open.**
    Do think before you act. Ask yourself how someone else might perceive what you are doing. If a student were to leave your classroom or other area and claim abuse, a closed area with no visual access would leave little room for a defense.

2. **Do not allow students to become overly friendly or familiar with you. Students should never call teachers by their first names or nicknames.**
    There is a difference between being "friendly" and being "friends" with students. Boundaries between adults and young persons must be enforced. Insisting on proper titles is one way to keep boundaries.

3. **Do not engage in private correspondence with students. If you receive personal communication from a student and the communication is not appropriate, keep a copy of the communication and do not respond unless you have received**

permission from a supervisor.
It is not uncommon for students to develop "crushes" on teachers, to fantasize about them, and/or to try to communicate on a peer level. If one receives student letters, etc., that are romantic, sexual, or otherwise inappropriate, it is best not to respond and to report the occurrence to one's supervisor for everyone's protection.

4. **Do not visit students in their homes unless their parents are present.**
Being alone with young persons can give an appearance of impropriety. Many accusations of sexual abuse are alleged to have occurred when adults were present in students' homes when the parents were absent. In particular, if there is no one home but the student, the situation can quickly become one of your word against the student's, if an allegation of misconduct is made.

5. **Do not invite students to your home.**
The same comments in #4 apply here.

6. **Do not transport students in your vehicle.**
Obviously, there exists the same problematic situation of an adult being alone with a student or students. In addition, the adult may assume personal liability for any accident or injury. It can be very tempting to respond to a student's request for a ride home, but a better approach would be to wait in an open area with the student until transportation arrives or to direct the student to an administrator.

7. **Do not take the role of surrogate parent with a student.**
Educators are not parents and do not have the responsibilities or privileges of parents. While

being supportive and helpful, educators must respect the rights of parents. Some parents, feeling teachers have displaced them in their children's affections, are seeking restraining orders against the educators.

8. Do not criticize a student's parents to the student.

No matter how poorly parents parent, they are most likely the only parents their children will have. If you believe a child is abused or neglected, contact the appropriate authorities.

9. Do not give students your home or cell phone number without the permission and knowledge of your supervisor.

While it is true that many teachers' numbers are listed in the phone book and are readily available, it is prudent to not give such information unless one's supervisor is informed. In the event of an allegation of abuse, the giving of one's personal phone numbers to students can raise a specter of questions.

10. Do not communicate with students from your home e-mail address.

The same reasons as offered in #9 above apply here. One should always communicate with students from one's school, rather than home e-mail address. If a teacher has a web page which students can access for academic reasons, it should be part of the school's web site and administrators should be able to access it at all times.

11. Do not hire students to work in your home without the express knowledge and consent of your supervisor.

In the past, many teachers regularly relied upon their students to provide such services as baby-sitting and grass cutting. The difficulty that can arise is again one of the appearance of impropriety. What defense will a male teacher who is driving a high school freshman home after babysitting have if she makes an allegation of inappropriate behavior? The roles of teacher and employer should not be mixed. Before taking any action, a good question to ask oneself is: *"How would I feel if what I am doing were to appear on the front page of the paper tomorrow?"*

The Internet & E-Mail

Other boundary issues are posed by the use of Internet and e-mail in Catholic schools. Students communicate routinely use the Internet and they expect to use it to communicate with teachers as well. Parents are requesting, even demanding, that they be able to access information about their children's academic performance via the Internet. With the best of intentions, a teacher can find him or herself accused of improper behavior in communications with students. Administrators can be accused of violations of privacy due to information posted on school websites.

School Websites

A growing number of schools are giving parents passwords and allowing them to access their children's academic records. Some schools are recording progress grades every few weeks. In some schools, teachers post all student grades on the Internet and a parent uses a password to view all the grades the student has received. These are perfectly acceptable practices that will continue.

People value their privacy. Parents have a right to expect that personal information, such as addresses and phone numbers that the school requires them to provide, will not be shared with others, even other parents, without their express or implied consent.

Administrators need to insure that:

(1) The school website is secure.

(2) Only persons with passwords may access student records and then only the records of their own children.

(3) School information should not violate privacy. For example, if the school administrators wish to publish the school directory with student and parent addresses and phone numbers, they should ensure that parents either give written permission to include such information or the school handbook states certain information will be published unless the parent notifies the school in writing by a certain date that such information should not be included for his or her family. Similarly, parents should have the right to request that their children's photos not be placed on the school's website.

E-mail Issues

E-mail and instant messaging are examples of the blessing and the curse that technology brings to schools. Teachers must understand that there is no privacy on the Internet. The same boundary issues that must be respected in oral communications with students must be respected in written ones, particularly when e-mail is involved. Many people may view what is written, so the test of publicity must always be kept in mind: *"How would I feel if this correspondence suddenly ended up on the front page of the newspaper or on the evening news?"* The following ten guidelines can help teachers and staff in the appropriate use of e-mail.

1. Use your school e-mail account. Never use your home or personal e-mail account. Using a personal account can give an appearance of secrecy.

2. Always remember you are a professional rendering a service to students. You are not the student's friend or buddy.

3. Communicate only about school matters or matters that are appropriate to be discussed in school. Most especially avoid any communication that might be construed as having sexual overtones. Do not reply to any such e-mail you receive from students; make and keep a copy of any such inappropriate communication and notify the principal.

4. Write as though you are certain that others will read what you write. Remember that a student can share your message with students and others by a simple push of a button.

5. Remember there is no such thing as a private e-mail.

6. Do not use instant messaging. Do not put students on your "buddy list." If you find that a student has added you to his or her list, ask that your name be removed and keep a written record of your request. Remember – people can make copies of instant messages and they can come back to haunt you. If you are involved in an academic chat room, use it appropriately.

7. Ask yourself: "If my principal or anyone asked to see this communication, would I be embarrassed by what I have written?" If the answer is "yes," don't send the e-mail.

8. Remember – the student you are e-mailing is someone's child. How would you feel if your child received the e-mail you are about to send? If you think your e-mail might somehow be misunderstood, don't send it.

9. Remember – boundaries must be respected in written correspondence as well as in oral communica-

tion. Don't push the boundaries of teacher/student relationships.

10. Finally, e-mail can be misinterpreted. Before sending an e-mail, ask yourself if someone reading it might "read something into it" that you didn't intend, or if your message might be misinterpreted. Communicate in person whenever possible.

Confidentiality:
What Can Be Told? What Should Be Told?

Teachers often ask about keeping the confidences of students who share information with them. They generally know that priests have a priest/penitent privilege that is respected in court. They may have heard that counselors and therapists have some sort of privilege, but they are not sure if courts recognize it. They may wonder if teachers have any legal protections when dealing with student confidences.

One of the more perplexing situations facing Catholic educators today is that presented by students sharing confidential information. Educators may have heard stories about teachers who failed to report student threats and the student subsequently acted on the threat. The responsibility for receiving the confidences of young persons and advising students in both day-to-day situations and crises can be overwhelming. Busy teachers, counselors, administrators, and even parent volunteers may well ask: *"What am I supposed to do? I know I'm not a professional counselor, a psychiatrist, or a social worker, but I'm the one the individual trusts, the one that was consulted. Are there certain legal issues involved in the receiving of confidences? Is there matter that must be made known to others, even when the person has asked for and received a promise of confidentiality from me?"*

These are good questions to ask. Educators cannot afford to think that they can help all persons all the time, for this is not possible. If, for example, a student were to come to a teacher or other staff member and say that he or she is experiencing shortness of breath and chest pain, the adult would quickly summon both the student's parents and medical assistance. Yet, psychological problems are no less serious than physical ones, and the layperson who attempts to deal with such problems unaided may well be courting tragedy for both oneself and the one confiding.

Confidentiality is generally held to mean that one individual or several individuals will keep private information that has been given to them and will not reveal it. For example, the person who receives the sacrament of reconciliation rightfully expects that the subject matter of confession will be held sacred by the confessor and will not be revealed to anyone. Indeed, there are accounts of priests who died rather than break the seal of confession.

Friends share confidences with each other. One individual may say to another: *"This is confidential; you cannot repeat it."* The person speaking in confidence has a right to expect that the confidant to whom the information has been given will keep the matter secret. But there are recognized limits to what friends will keep private. If one's friend confides that she has been stockpiling sleeping medication and plans to take all of it that evening so as to commit suicide, it is not hard to see that morality demands that the confidant communicate that knowledge to a spouse or other family member of the confiding individual, or take some other action that would intervene in the attempted suicide.

It is not unheard of for an adult who would not hesitate to get help for a friend to believe that a young person who is talking about suicide is not serious, or can be talked out of the planned action, or is not capable of carrying out a threatened suicide. As child and adolescent psychologists report, young people often do not think through the long-term ramifications of suicide attempts. There is also, among some young people, a fascination with death, as can be seen by the idolization of famous people who have died young or committed suicide.

If a student tells a teacher or other staff member that he or she is going to harm self or others, the adult must reveal that information, even if a promise of confidentiality has been given. In a number of lawsuits brought against teachers and school districts, parents sought damages from teachers who were told by students in confidence that they planned to harm themselves or others. The teachers did not contact parents or other authorities and the students carried through with the threatened harm. In some cases, the educators were brought to trial on a claim of negligence by failure to warn.

School shootings and related violence have resulted in a flurry of litigation. Parents of the victims of various school shootings have brought suit against school districts, schools, administrators, and teachers; some suits allege that journals and writings of the perpetrators contained warning signals that school staff members disregarded. The litigation may continue for years; regardless of which side "wins," the case fallout will be enormous in terms of student and community trust. Such cases also cause teachers to question the wisdom of journal writing and, indeed, any writing that may involve personal thoughts and feelings.

Counselor Immunity

It is a widely held myth that counselors, physicians, psychologists, and social workers have legal immunity from responsibility for any injuries that may arise from failing to act on confidential information presented to them. Most states have abolished counselor immunity and the few who still "have it on the books" have imposed several limitations on the concept. A counselor who hears from a person that the individual plans to kill his or her parents and does nothing about it will not be legally able to decline to answer questions under oath, nor will the counselor be held harmless for any resulting injuries if he or she decides not to reveal the threats. Teachers must understand that, while they are teaching their classes, they are generally not considered counselors. Counselors themselves must understand that they have very little protection if they fail to make potentially harmful confidences known. Thus, counselors, teachers, and other staff members must make it very clear to a confiding individual that they will keep confidences unless the individual's health, life, or safety, or those of another are threatened. Administrators should seriously consider the development of a policy that directs adult staff members to tell individuals at the outset: *"I will keep your confidences so long as no one's life, health, or safety is involved. Once life, health, or safety is involved, I cannot promise confidentiality."* The only two privileges from disclosure of confidential information, which seem to remain in state law, are that of priest/penitent and attorney/client.

In light of the above, teachers must presume that no legal protection exists for those who receive confidences. What can be expected of a teacher who wants to be a role model for young persons, who wants to be approachable and helpful? The answer is simple: Lay down the ground rules for confidentiality before receiving any confidences. If a student asks to talk to a teacher in confidence, the teacher should reiterate the ground rules before the sharing begins.

Journal Writing

In religion, language arts, English, and other subjects, teachers have long recognized the value of student journal writing. This practice does, however, carry a real risk of disclosure of information that the teacher is compelled to reveal. All must set the same rules for confidentiality discussed above.

Today, teachers must understand that they *are* expected to read what students write. If a teacher cannot read the assignment, then the assignment should not be given. In particular, techniques, such as telling students to clip together pages they do not wish the adult to read or to write at the top of such pages: *"Please do not read,"* should be avoided. Journal writing has a place in today's schools, but the teachers must be sure that all students understand the parameters of the assignment and the responsibilities for reporting threatened danger. Administrators, teachers, and volunteers should discuss the concept of journalling and develop policies and procedures to ensure that journals are used appropriately.

Teachers who do not use the journal writing technique may believe that they are "off the hook" with journal issues. However, many teachers have found themselves on the receiving end of written student confidences. A student may write the teacher a note on the bottom of an assignment sheet. Students choose teachers they trust when deciding to whom to confide personal information. Anyone who teaches children or adolescents must reflect on the special responsibilities the receiving of confidences imposes and be prepared to respond appropriately when potentially harmful information is communicated.

Retreats

The retreat experience is designed to be a valuable spiritual experience for students. However, young people are often at their most vulnerable in such situations. They may share stories of child abuse, sexual harassment, family dysfunction, and even possible criminal activity. While encouraging sharing, the teacher/group leader must once again set the ground rules before the sharing beings. The use of peer leaders (often utilized even at the grade school level) does not lessen the responsibility of the supervising adults. Student leaders must be told of the ground rules and of the necessity to communicate them to group members as well as procedures to be followed in notifying adults if matter is revealed that must be reported.

A second problematic area posed by retreats and written communication is the increasing practice of significant adults, such as parents and teachers, writing letters to retreatants.

While it is appropriate to express good wishes and prayers for the student retreatant, teachers should be careful to avoid statements that could be perceived as overly "personal." For example, a teacher should not write: *"I love you, Tom,"* and then sign the letter. The teacher may very well be referring to a generic type of love, but the student's parent might read something different into the statement. The best practice for all teachers is to assume that nothing is confidential and to ask oneself if what one is doing or writing will pass the test of "publication," i.e., being seen and judged by others.

Case Law

In the 1995 case, *Brooks v. Logan and Joint District No. 2*, the parents of a student who had committed suicide filed an action for wrongful death and a claim for negligent infliction of emotional distress against a teacher who had assigned the keeping of journals to her class. Jeff Brooks was a student at Meridian High School and was assigned to Ms. Logan's English class. Students were asked to make entries into a daily journal as part of their English composition work. For a period of four months prior to his death, Jeff wrote in his journal.

After his death, Ms. Logan read through the entries and gave the journal to a school counselor, who delivered it to Jeff's parents. Jeff had made journal entries that indicated that he was depressed and that he was contemplating suicide. Ms. Logan maintained that Jeff had requested that she not read his entries, so that he would feel free to express himself. The journal contained a note in which Ms. Logan stated that she would not read the journal for content, but would only check for dates and length. The parents maintained that, in a conversation with Ms. Logan after their receipt of the journal, she stated that she had "reread the entries." Ms. Logan denied that she made that statement, and contends that she did not read the entries in question until after Jeff's death.

The lower court granted summary judgment in favor of the

teacher and the school district. However, the appellate court reversed the finding, and held that there were issues of fact in existence, which could only be determined at trial. Thus, a trial court was directed to determine whether Ms. Logan's actions or inactions constituted negligence contributing to Jeff's death. The court was directed to make a determination as to whether Jeff's suicide was foreseeable: would a reasonable person in Ms. Logan's place have recognized the possibility of suicide and notified someone? The appellate court refers to similar case law in which jailers have been held liable for the suicide of prisoners when the prisoners had exhibited warning signs.

This case demonstrates the vulnerability of teachers who receive student confidences. Administrators should discuss the topic of confidentiality with their staffs and adopt policies that will support a legally sound approach to confidentiality. The wise teacher will establish and enforce ground rules and boundaries for dealing with student confidences, and will seek help from others when appropriate.

Note: An Example of a Boundaries Policy

In the author's work with schools, she occasionally encounters a policy or document that might serve as a model for other schools. With the permission of the President of Catholic Memorial High School (West Roxbury Massachusetts), Brother James MacDonald, C.F.C., the author includes their policy, *"Establishing Boundaries between Catholic Memorial Employees/Volunteers and Students"* in an appendix following Chapter VII.

Violence: What Can Catholic Schools Do?

The all too frequent headline: *"Student Kills Other Students,"* elicits from some Catholic educators a sigh of relief that such events have not happened in their schools. However, only the most naïve person would think that such violence could occur only in public schools. While all educators devoutly hope that they will never be faced with such a terrible situation, they should realize that they must prepare for threatened and actual violence

Most Catholic educational administrators have at least considered the need for policies and procedures that would deal with student violence. But some have decided that it is better to wait until the unthinkable happens rather than to begin planning ways of dealing with it. However, as many administrators have learned to their chagrin, it is far better easier to write a policy that you never use, than to try to write one to cover a present situation. Attempting to write policies after the fact leaves the alleged offender believing that he or she is being personally singled out for punishment. Every school should have in place mechanisms for the threat, or actual occurrence of violence.

What Should Be in the Policy?

First, school officials, teachers, and board members must agree on a definition of violence. It is not necessary to use a legal definition, such as one gleaned from legal texts, but the definition should be clear to the average reader. Violence can be defined as causing physical harm to another. Such a definition should also include threatened violence: threatened violence is defined as threatening to cause physical harm to another. While this definition does not deal with emotional or verbal abuse, or other non-tangible injuries, it is, nonetheless, a clear definition of violence.

This author has heard from many educators across the country who are developing appropriate policies and procedures. An often-asked question is: *"Should we have zero tolerance for violence and threats of violence?"* One mother of a five-year-old kindergarten student stated that the principal had told the kindergarten class that anyone who said: *"I'm going to kill you,"* would be suspended and possibly expelled. The

mother was aghast that any principal would threaten such dras-
tic action to a five year old, who may well have heard otherwise good people, including adults, use such language. But the
sad fact is that desperate times, as the saying goes, call for
desperate measures. *"How would you, as a mother feel,"* the
author asked, *"if a classmate made such a threat to your child,
and then returned to class the next day with some sort of
weapon and frightened or harmed your child? Wouldn't you
want something done?"* The mother admitted that, yes, she
would expect that the threatening child would receive some
punishment.

So, should there be a zero tolerance policy for threatened
or actual violence? The answer is "yes." But zero tolerance can
have more than one meaning. A kindergarten child should not
be expelled for making such a statement. Many people believe
that older students, including high school students, should be
given a second chance. While agreeing that very young children should not be severely disciplined, the author suggests
that there be a range of remedies according to age. For example, kindergarten and other primary grade students making
threats might result in a parent/teacher/principal/student
conference in which all parties are made aware that any subsequent threats will result in suspension and required counseling
before the student will be allowed to return to school. Older
elementary students might be suspended and referred to counseling on the first offense. A second offense could result in
dismissal from school. Actual violence will result in stiffer
penalties. Depending on the situation, a student could be
expelled or suspended for a long period of time and re-admit-
ted only after counselor clearance. Definitions and penalties
should be very clear. If a school does not have a policy, now is
the time to write one. Since schools generally require parents
to sign statements that they have read and agree to be governed
by the school, parents in signing have agreed to all policies,
including ones concerning threatened or actual violence.

Educators should explain the policy in detail, as appropriate by grade level. Examples of unacceptable behavior should be given. Some schools have had great success with teachers and/or parents presenting skits. In any case, strong instruction and direction should be given.

What about secondary students? High school administrators seem to be divided in responses to student violence. Many schools simply expel on the first offense. Such an approach is clean and clear, although to some, it may seem very harsh. Other administrators permit a student to be reinstated after serving a suspension and presenting a counselor's or doctor's note recommending re-admittance and stating that the student does not pose a threat. Actual violence should normally result in dismissal from school. Administrators should ensure that students know exactly what behavior is forbidden, especially since the penalty is so severe.

No matter how cautious and fair educators are, there will be some cases with extreme mitigating factors. A school handbook that states: *"The principal (and/or pastor) is the final recourse in all disciplinary situations and may waive any and all regulations for just cause at his or her discretion."* Such a statement gives the administrator the room for some discretion, if discretion should ever be needed.

Harassment and Bullying

Teachers and administrators are not the only members of the school community who must be concerned with boundary issues. Students are required to respect the privacy and personal space of others. Unfortunately, that respect is not always forthcoming; two examples of such lack of respect are harassment and bullying. While persons are generally aware of issues surrounding sexual harassment, issues related to non-sexual harassment, including bullying, are less clear.

One may well ask: *"What exactly is harassment? We talk about it a great deal, but I've yet to see a good, general defi-*

nition." The ultimate legal authority for definitions is *Black's Law Dictionary* which defines harassment as:

> Used in variety of legal contexts to describe words, gestures and actions which tend to annoy, alarm and abuse another person. A person commits a petty misdemeanor if, with purpose to harass another, he: (1) makes a telephone call without purpose of legitimate communication; or (2) insults, taunts or challenges another in a manner likely to promote a disorderly response; or (3) makes repeated communications anonymously or at extremely inconvenient hours, or in offensively coarse language; or (4) subjects another to an offensive touching; or (5) engages in any other course of alarming conduct serving no legitimate purpose of the actor.

Harassment occurs, then, when one person makes repeated verbal or physical contacts with another person who does not want these contacts. Sexual harassment is a particular type of harassment that involves sexual comments, innuendo, invitations and/or requests for sexual favors. Sexual harassment is generally fairly clear; other types of harassment can be more blurred and may be harder to identify.

Bullying is a type of harassment that involves some sort of force, whether overt or subtle. For example, today exclusion is widely considered to be a form of bullying, even though there may be no apparent contact. By ignoring and/or excluding an individual from participation, the bully shows his or her power.

The real problem in harassment cases is a failure to respect the dignity of another. Since there are many ways to exhibit disrespect, administrators would be well advised to consider having a rule that simply forbids all demeaning behavior. There is a place, of course, for more detailed listings of possible offenses, but more general "catch all" clauses ensure that most inappropriate behaviors can "be caught" and persons held accountable under the more general provision.

Under the previously cited doctrine of respondeat superior, let the superior answer, teachers and other supervisors can be held liable for one young person's harassment or bullying of another. If a teacher or other educator knows or has been informed that one student is harassing another and fails to act, the teacher can be held liable for the harassment. Although the majority of such cases involve sexual harassment, the potential for liability for other types of harassment exists as well. Thus, students exhibiting demeaning behaviors must be immediately corrected.

Educators really have five main duties in these areas, which can be placed under the broad, general category of demeaning behavior. They are:

(1) **the duty to minimize risks:** teachers should periodically examine practices and routines to see if there are times and places when bullying and harassment are more likely to occur and should then make plans to minimize the likelihood of occurrence.

(2) **the duty to educate students:** teachers need to show in word and deed that demeaning behavior is not appropriate.

(3) **the duty to investigate complaints and concerns:** if a student expresses discomfort, the educator should carefully investigate the situation, while remembering that things may not always be what they seem.

(4) **the duty to remedy violations:** Teachers should swiftly and firmly correct students who engage in demeaning behaviors.

(5) **the duty to monitor students and situations:** Teachers should remember the old "eyes in the back of the head" image and pay careful attention to students at all times.

Teachers often ask for practical suggestions in meeting legal responsibilities. Knowledge of law and legal phrases is of little use if one cannot put the ethical principles that drive the law into practice. The following are ten suggestions.

Prevention and Intervention Techniques
1. Create a climate where all students are valued.
2. Observe students at times when you're not "in charge."
3. Watch for the warning signs of isolation, depression, and suppressed anger.
4. Err on the side of caution when expressing concerns about student behaviors and attitudes.
5. Do not keep secrets.
6. Tell students that you will keep confidences only if health, life, safety, and/or criminal activity are not at issue.
7. When assigning students to groups, use random methods rather than self-selection.
8. Do not allow name-calling or demeaning comments.
9. Listen to what students don't say as well as to what they do say.
10. Remember that supervision is a *mental* as well as a *physical* act.

Hazing

One form of bullying and harassment that has been present in schools for many years is hazing. Readers may well have been subjected to some form of hazing when they were in school, even if it was called by other names such as "initiation," or "rites of passage."

Hazing, a particular form of harassment, has been around schools for a long time. Most readers have probably experienced hazing in some form in their school careers, although it may have masqueraded under the title of initiation and may have seemed fairly harmless: requiring students to wear signs stating: *"I am a lowly freshman,"* or *"I am the slave of the varsity basketball team,"* or forbidding students to use a certain set of stairs and/or making them take a longer way to get to their classrooms.

Other forms of hazing are present in schools. The student who "forces" another student to steal items from a grocery store or face some dire consequence is bullying the individual. When that kind of behavior is required as "payment" for belonging to a team or club, hazing is occurring. Some hazing, though, has escalated out of all control as students have suffered severe injuries and even death.

StopHazing, an excellent organization with its own website at StopHazing.org, has defined hazing as:

"Hazing" refers to any activity expected of someone joining a group (or to maintain full status in a group) that humiliates, degrades or risks emotional and/or physical harm, regardless of the person's willingness to participate….Hazing is a complex social problem that is shaped by power dynamics operating in a group and/or organization and within a particular cultural context.

Today, many forms of hazing are being reported from relatively simple ones to such activities as: burning, branding, paddling, depriving persons of sleep and food, forcing individuals to drink alcohol, often in large amounts, and compelling persons to engage in unreasonable amounts of physical exercise, to name a few. Some "popular" high school hazing activities today involve such actions as slapping an initiate on the arm, leg, thigh, or stomach until the body part turns red, forcing a student to urinate in public, forcing a student to put his or head in a toilet, and requiring a student to eat until he or she "throws up."

Administrators, athletic directors, coaches, teachers, and moderators need to pay close attention to student activities, "talk" and the proverbial rumor mill. If students are talking about hazing activities, the administration needs to be informed and an investigation begun.

Teachers, other supervisors, and even team captains can be held liable for one young person's harassment, bullying and/or hazing of another if they knew or should have known about it. Including hazing in the list of prohibited behaviors may raise awareness.

Health Issues and the Law

Although persons in Catholic schools do not have the same Constitutional protections as those in the public sector, statutory laws such as health regulations can bind individuals in both the public and the private sector. Administrators should carefully read all health-related communications from state or local agencies. Administrators who should have known what the law was will be held to the same standard that persons who know the law are required to meet.

Planning

The first step in planning should be identification of any existing health or safety problems that can be remedied. Inviting everyone in the school community to list problematic areas can aid in issue identification. Health and safety issues are related; failure to meet safety needs can result in health-related problems. A broken bleacher can result in a person's breaking a leg or arm. Courts expect that administrators will be proactive in identifying potential safety problems. At least once a year a complete safety audit of the entire building(s) should be undertaken.

Staff Members and Health Issues

Staff members may be required to produce documentation of health and/or a doctor's statement that the person will not pose a health threat for the community. For example, tuberculosis, a communicable disease, poses a distinct threat. State law may require new teachers to have a tuberculin skin test and/or a chest X-ray to rule out the presence of tuberculosis before the teacher starts work.

Universal Precautions

Staff members should always use universal precautions whenever body fluids are present. If universal precautions are used, there is no reason for a supervising adult to refuse to deal with blood or other body fluids. No employee or volunteer dealing with children should be permitted to refuse to clean up body fluids or to render aid to a bleeding student. Clear procedures will help to ensure a calm, sound approach to situations involving body fluids.

The legal principle, often applied in negligence cases: *"the younger the child chronologically or mentally, the greater the standard of care,"* applies in body fluid situations. Supervisors of small children are held to a higher standard; however, those who supervise older students are still held to the standard of taking whatever action a reasonable person would take.

Storing and Dispensing Medication

Every administrator has dealt, at one time or the other, with the problems of storing and dispensing student medication. In many elementary schools, a designated person, such as the nurse or secretary, may be responsible for storing and dispensing medication. In other schools, the task may be assigned to classroom teachers. High schools may expect students to be responsible for self-administering all medication.

Attorneys can identify problems with almost any approach. Whenever an educator or volunteer administers medication, he or she may be liable for any reaction which occurs. One dangerous policy allows parents to bring over-the-counter medications with the student's name written on them to the school so that they can be stored and given to the student as needed. The difficulty is that persons are having increasing problems with reactions to non-prescription medication and a student could have a serious medical emergency after ingesting an over-the-counter medication. If parents are allowed to bring over the counter medication, the school should insist on written permission from both parent and physician.

The following statements offer some points to consider when policies and procedures are being determined.

(1.) The only persons who have an absolute right to the administration of medication are those who have serious chronic and/or life-threatening illnesses. For example, those who are allergic to bee stings must have the antidote serum readily available. A diabetic must be able to have prescribed insulin injections. Diabetics can, of course, be taught to administer and monitor their own medication; those allergic to bees most often need someone else to inject the antidote.

(2.) At least two persons must be identified who will be/are trained in the administration of injections or other drugs that a person cannot administer on her own.

(3.) Children and adolescents must be allowed to carry medication for life threatening attacks. Asthma is one condition that may give no warning; if an inhaler is not immediately available, the student could be severely harmed.

(4.) Adults who administer medication must place their whole attention on the task. The proper paper work should be present, e.g., a prescription label in the student's name, a doctor's note of authorization, and a parent's written permission.

(5.) If a teacher has a student with a life-threatening disease, the teacher must learn how to administer the medication. This reality is a matter of law, not choice.

(6.) Young children should not be responsible for oral medication, other than inhalers. Oral medication should be brought to and kept in the office.

(7.) High school-age persons may be allowed to carry and monitor their own non-prescription medication, so long as the parent/student handbook contains a statement to that effect.

Allergies and Allergic Reactions: Legal Responsibilities?

Closely related to the question of medication is the issue of allergies and the school's responsibility to students with allergies. More students than ever have allergies and parents request administrators to:

(1) take appropriate measures to prevent exposure to allergens;

(2) keep and store medication;

(3) learn how to provide emergency medical treatment for allergic reactions; and,

(4) educate students and, indeed, the entire school community, to the nature of allergic reactions.

Some staff members express fear or unwillingness to render aid to students experiencing allergic reactions. Teachers may ask if they "have to" assume such responsibility. Administrators may be concerned about liability.

Are Students with Allergies Protected by Disability Law?

Yes. A disability can generally be defined as any condition that interferes with one or more life activities. Persons with certain food allergies or allergies to bee stings can experience life-threatening allergic reactions. Students with allergies may be considered as having disabilities covered by Section 504 of the Rehabilitation Act of 1973 (amended 1974) which prohibits educational programs receiving federal funds from discriminating against otherwise qualified students if, with reasonable accommodation, they can meet the school's requirements. Thus, students who need injections of adrenaline, for example, are protected. A student who cannot eat peanut butter or nuts is protected.

In 2004, the United States Office of Civil Rights held that a Brockton, Massachusetts, Catholic elementary school violated Section 504 when it refused admission to a kindergarten child with a severe peanut allergy whose parents requested a *peanut free classroom*. The school paid a settlement equal to the difference between its tuition and that of the private school the child attended. OCR required that it monitor compliance for the following three years.

Must Such Students be Admitted to Catholic Schools and Programs? Why?

Some school and diocesan administrators are receiving requests from parents of students who are not allergic to certain foods, such as peanuts, that students who are allergic not be allowed to enroll in the school. The request seems to stem from the school's limitation of types of snacks that can be brought to school for parties and sometimes what is served in the cafeteria. Since federal law protects such students, they cannot be refused admission simply on the basis of having an allergy that may inconvenience other students and/or their parents.

What About the Rights of Parents of Students Who are Not Allergic? Can the School Impose and Must These Parents Follow Restrictions Because a Few Students Have Allergies?

Parents of non-allergic students must comply with school directives to refrain from sending snacks with peanuts or other allergens to their children's classes. They may have to accept that peanut butter or items with peanuts or items processed in plants where peanuts are processed may not be served in the cafeteria. These are simply reasonable accommodations. In one case, the parents of one student with the peanut allergy requested that no one be allowed to bring peanut products of any kind into the school. When contacted by an administrator in that school system, the author advised requiring the parent to produce a doctor's statement listing exactly what accommodations were necessary. A parent might believe that his/her child would be safest in a peanut-free environment, but if there is no medical necessity for that accommodation, the school is not obligated to make it. Thus, a school does not have to make every accommodation, but only reasonable ones that are medically necessary. In one case, a student may need a completely peanut free environment; in another, he or she may only need to avoid the allergen.

These situations present opportunities for compassion. In discussing restrictions with parents, administrators should stress not only the legal requirements, but also the Gospel imperatives of "loving one's neighbor as oneself" and the importance of "doing unto others as you would have them do unto you."

What are Teachers and Administrators Required to Do?

Teachers and administrators must do whatever is necessary to reasonably accommodate students with disabilities. A student must be allowed to carry an Epi-Pen if needed and the teacher must administer the injection if necessary. Failure to do so could result in serious injury to, or the death of, the student. Squeamishness must be set aside. Whatever a parent would reasonably do for a child, a teacher must do.

The following is a list of legal "do's and don'ts" when dealing with student allergies.

(1) Students cannot be refused admission or continued enrollment simply on the basis of their having allergies to food, insects, or other substances.

(2) Reasonable accommodations must be made.

(3) If other students and parents are inconvenienced by the accommodations, they must accept the inconvenience.

(4) Educators must be willing to learn about the allergies and the treatment needed.

(5) Educators must be willing to administer medication when needed.

(6) Educators should not isolate such students or take actions that might separate the student from other students or activities without parental permission.

(7) Remind everyone that in every situation, all should act as Jesus would.

Students With Special Needs: What Should A Catholic School Do?

The last several years have seen a sharp increase in threatened litigation against Catholic schools because students with special needs are seeking admission and/or retention.

Section 504 of the Rehabilitation Act of 1973 (amended 1974) and the 1992 Americans with Disabilities Act may seem puzzling to the non-lawyer. Myths and half-truths abound. Some consultants and lawyers advise that schools and church buildings must be made totally accessible. Many board members and administrators fear that the cost of accommodations will be so high as to force schools and parish programs out of existence. Some school and program administrators question accepting students with special needs. Can the average Catholic school or parish provide the proper program adjustments needed by these students? Board members, as well Catholic school and program personnel, need a clear understanding of legal requirements.

Education Access Laws

As stated previously in this text, federal law prohibits discrimination on the basis of race, sex, disability, age, and national origin. Board members and administrators must understand the law governing students with special needs in schools. Public Law 94-142, The Education of All Handicapped Children Act, and its successor law, The Individuals with Disabilities in Education Act, ensure a "free and appropriate education" for all children. There is no requirement that Catholic schools provide the "free and appropriate education." However, in situations in which the only school for the handicapped/disabled is one operated by the Catholic Church or some other private organization, the state may place a child in a private school if that placement seems to provide the most appropriate education. In such a case, the state would be responsible for the tuition.

Catholic schools are not required to meet every need of every child. Most Catholic schools are not equipped to offer all educational services to everyone. The fact that a school does not have to offer services does not mean that a student attending that school has no right to such services. The public school must make every reasonable effort to provide the student with services needed, even if the student remains in the Catholic school. If it is not practical to offer such services to a Catholic school student, the public school officials can draw up an individual education plan (IEP) that calls for public school education. A parent is always free to accept or reject such an IEP. If a parent elects to keep a child in a private school over the objections of the professional educators working with that child, the public school cannot be held responsible for the child's progress, nor can the public school be required to pay private school tuition.

It is important to note that the private school student and the public school student have the same federal protections. The private school student has a right to the same services a public school student is entitled to receive; however, the private school student may not be able to insist that the services be provided within a private school as part of an IEP.

Standards of Supervision

Administrators, many of whom are familiar with the adage: *"the younger the child chronologically or mentally, the greater the standard of care,"* may ask: *"If we accept students with special needs, are we committing ourselves to higher levels of supervision?"*

Mental age is concerned with the effect that a disability may have on a child. If a Catholic school or program accepts a student with a mental disability, teachers and other supervisors must make reasonable accommodations. If a child performs well below grade level and exhibits immature behavior, a teacher may be expected to provide more stringent supervision than that given to other students. Some disabilities are not mental, of course. If a child is an amputee, the child will require more supervision and help in physical activities than others may need.

If a student with special needs is denied admission to a Catholic school, the possibility of liability is always present. Surely the more important question is: *"How would Jesus want us to treat persons with special needs?"* Discussion of this question can be difficult, particularly in the light of rising costs and limited personnel. All involved in Catholic education need to examine their institutional responses to special needs.

Discipline

All students need to be accountable to persons in authority and special needs children are no exception. Schools and parishes have the right to require that all students abide by codes of conduct. Every person in a Catholic institution should be expected to obey the rules.

Exceptions are in order only when the infraction is the result of the disability. If students who use walkers or crutches cannot get to class on time because they simply cannot move fast enough, it would be unfair to penalize them for being late. Another example is presented by a student with Tourette's syndrome, which is often characterized by bizarre behavior, such as swearing. If a student suffering from Tourette's were to use profanity, it would be unfair to discipline the student if the behavior is beyond the student's control.

No federal or state law requires that institutions create programs to meet the needs of the disabled. What the law requires is that institutions not discriminate against otherwise qualified persons who are seeking admission to their programs. If a disabled person can attend the school and make satisfactory progress with a reasonable amount of accommodation, then the institution must provide the accommodation. If providing that accommodation would create a significant hardship, the institution will not have to provide it. For example, if a blind student were to seek admission and acceptance of that student would require that a special teacher be employed for the student and that all teachers learn Braille, the school would probably not be expected to incur those expenses.

It must be frankly stated, however, that simply because one is *not* legally required to do something, it does not follow that one should not do that thing, if it is the right thing to do. If a school has significant assets and could afford a sign language interpreter for a deaf student or instructions in signing for the faculty and staff, the administrator may have a moral and ethical duty to provide for the student, even though the law does not require such provision. Indeed, the Pastoral Statement of U.S. Catholic Bishops on Handicapped People (1978) seems to demand such action: *"If handicapped people are to become equal partners in the Christian community, injustices must be eliminated."* Certainly, Catholic parishes and schools should be leaders in fighting injustice wherever it is found, especially as it affects those whose disabilities place them among persons for whom Christ manifested special concern.

The Right to the Best Education

Federal law gives all students the right to a "free and appropriate education." Students must be evaluated for special services at parental request, but the law does not entitle students to a special needs program. Catholic school students have the same right to evaluation as do public school students. However, the program recommended as a result of the evaluation may not be available in the Catholic school, which is required only to make reasonable accommodations.

Discrimination law does not require that the education be the best available. To require the best education would mean that school systems would constantly be meeting parental demands for instructional services that could "better" student performance.

As a result of the *D'Agostino* case that overturned the 1985 *Aguilar* decision, public schools can now provide services in religious schools. The key word is *can* which is not synonymous with *must*. Thus, public schools could still refuse to provide services in the Catholic school, so long as the students had access to them in the public school.

Much apprehension could be alleviated if administrators clearly understood what the law does and does not require. In the final analysis, though, the question is not: *"Did you do what you had to do?"* but *"Did you do what you could?"*

Special needs children and adolescents are certainly worthy of the Catholic Church's time and attention. It is a sad reality that only a few schools and parishes make adequate provisions for meeting the needs of such children. As persons striving to live in harmony with the Gospel, all involved in Catholic education are bound to do their utmost to assist students with special needs.

Two suggestions seem appropriate with regard to special education in the day-to-day operation of a school or program. Administrators should treat parents the way they would want to be treated if they had special needs children. No parent should ever be told on the telephone or by letter: *"Sorry, there's no place for your child here."* At the very least, administrators should offer to meet with such parents and discuss the situation. Even if a particular school cannot accommodate a child's needs, the administration will have expressed Christian concern.

Another suggestion is that all school administrators commit to undertaking an analysis of their programs' ability to meet special needs. An inability to meet special needs is not synonymous with inconvenience.

Jesus ordered his disciples: *"Let the children come to me. For such is the kingdom of heaven."* Such is the mission of all Catholic educators – to be as inclusive as Jesus was.

Issues of Custody

Custodial rights are much more of a challenge to educators today than at any other time. Researchers report that less than fifty per cent of children live with both biological parents. While the parents can certainly experience difficulties, it is the child who gets caught in the middle of parents and other relatives who disagree over custody.

Which parent does the law favor?

Contrary to popular belief, there is no law that mandates that mothers should be given preference in custody battles. Certainly, historically mothers have been favored in custody disputes. While mothers do tend to retain custody more often than fathers do, the law requires the judge to do what is in the best interests of the child. It must be noted, however, that two reasonable, intelligent justices can come to two different conclusions about what a child's best interests are. Therefore, no one can predict the outcome of a custody battle. Nonetheless, the guiding principle must be the best interests of the child.

Judges require that social workers and other advocates conduct detailed, painstaking studies of the environments available to the child and offer recommendations to the court. The process can be time-consuming. Childcare and child service providers can find themselves caught on the horns of the dilemma when separation occurs and/or divorce proceedings have begun: Which parent has the greater right? Further questions arise when other relatives – aunts, uncles, and grandparents – become involved and ask a child service provider or administrator to intervene or to take a particular action.

Everyone who provides services for young persons that require supervision of the children in the absence of the parents must remember that, unless altered by the court, both parents have rights. One cannot simply defer to the wishes of the parent one knows best or the parent one considers to be the more responsible. When a separation agreement is in place, it should be followed or the principal can simply call the judge and ask for help. Parents can be required to furnish the school or parish with a court-certified copy of the custody section of the separation agreement or divorce decree. In the absence of any of the above, administrators must assume that both parents have custodial rights.

What Does the Law Say About Parents Who are Separated, But Not Yet Divorced?

The law requires that each parent's rights be recognized. So, if a mother comes to the principal or teacher and states that she is going to leave her husband and she wants him to have no contract with the children, the minister or administrator must insist that a court-certified document be given to the parish or school which clearly states that the father is to be given no access to, or information concerning, his children before the wishes of the mother can be honored. While the rule of law is often clear, its application may be problematic. If a mother comes and states that she is terrified for her and her children's safety, the administrator must use common sense. No principal who believes a mother's fear of abuse is going to release a child into the custody of the father without proper legal authorization. Of course, allegations of abuse can be made on both sides. In such situations, the administrator should contact local police and the diocesan or parish attorney. Child Protective Services may also be contacted. Once a separation or divorce decree is given, officials should comply with its directives.

What are a Non-Custodial Parent's Rights to Access Information About the Child?

In the school setting, the Buckley Amendment provides clear guidelines governing access to academic progress information. By extension and through local laws and regulations, administrators should follow the guidelines of the Buckley Amendment in dealing with non-school cases. The Buckley Amendment of 1975 clearly gives non-custodial parents rights in regard to the academic performance of their children. Unless a court has ruled otherwise, non-custodial parents have the right to copies of their children's academic records, although address and other identifying information can be excluded. The non-custodial parent also has a right to discuss his or child's progress with school personnel. While a school official may be required to provide access to each parent, it may not be necessary to hold duplicate conferences. The administrator may decide to require a joint conference. Caution is in order in such situations. If one parent has a restraining order against the other, a joint conference cannot be held. Although it may be inconvenient to provide duplicate services, the educator must keep in mind that the primary responsibility ethically, even if not absolutely legally required, is to protect the child and his or her interests. If a child's interests appear to be best served by separate conferences, the administrator should provide them.

How Can a Policy That Will Govern Custody Situations be Constructed?

School officials, relying on the Buckley Amendment, can place a statement such as this in its parent/student handbook: *"The school abides by the provisions of the Buckley Amendment. Thus, non-custodial parents will be given access to the academic records and to information regarding the academic progress of their children, unless there is a court order specifically stating that the non-custodial parent is denied access to such information."*

Another approach is to require that all separated and divorced parents provide the school with a court-certified copy of the custody section of the appropriate decree. If the parent is to be denied access to the child's academic records, that denial should be noted in this section. The custody section should also provide information about the non-custodial parent's right of access to the child: for example, may the parent call for the child at school on the Friday's preceding weekend visitation?

All school administrators would be well-advised to gather as much data as possible concerning separated and divorced parents and their custodial rights and privileges, so that all will act in the best interests of the child and in a manner that is recognized by civil law.

Copyright Law

Most persons realize that copyright law exists. If asked, many would probably respond that there are rules that should be followed when making copies of articles, book chapters, computer programs, and television programs. Teachers and other staff members have seen notices warning persons using copy machines that they are subject to the provisions of the copyright law.

For some individuals, the fact that apprehension and prosecution for breaking the copyright law rarely become reality becomes a license to break the law. For others, their motive of helping students and young people learn is an excuse for failing to comply with the law.

Reasons to copy

In the 1960s and 1970s, budgetary considerations were the reasons given by Catholic churches that copied songs from copyrighted works and used the copies to compile parish hymnals. Courts have consistently struck down such uses and have ordered the offending churches to pay damages. Today, parishes appear to be aware of the legal consequences of copying and many subscribe to the licensing arrangements of music companies: for a given sum of money, the institution can make as many copies of music as desired during the span of the contract.

However, some teachers still copy such items as whole workbooks, other consumable materials, large portions of books, and print materials. The swift advance of technology has catapulted computer programs, videocassettes, CDs, DVDs, and similar media into the sphere of copying.

Upon reflection, most administrators and teachers would agree that copyright protection is a just law. The Copyright Act of 1976 attempts to safeguard the rights of authors. Persons who create materials are entitled to the fruits of their labors; those who use author's creations without paying royalties, buying copies, or seeking permission are guilty of stealing.

It is tempting to think that copyright infringements and lawsuits are more or less the exclusive domain of large institutions. Certainly, the public learns about large-scale abuses faster than individual abuses. Obviously if a company is going to sue someone, it will seek a person or institution that has been guilty of multiple infringements so that larger damages can be won. It simply doesn't make good economic sense to sue someone who will be ordered to pay only a small amount of damages.

Sometimes, though, lawsuits are brought solely to prove a point. A 1983 case, *Marcus v. Rowley*, involved a dispute between two teachers in the same school. One teacher had prepared and copyrighted a 20-page booklet on cake decorating; the second teacher copied approximately half the pages and included them in her own materials. The amount of money involved was negligible; the author had sold fewer than 100 copies at a price of $2. Nonetheless, the court found the second teacher guilty of copyright violation; her use of the other's materials was not "fair."

What is Fair Use?

Section 107 of the 1976 Copyright Act deals with "fair use" and specifically states that the fair use of copies in teaching "is not an infringement of copyright."

The "sticking point" is what the term "fair use" means. The section lists four factors to be included in any determination of fair use:

- the purpose and character of the use, including whether such use is of a commercial nature or is for nonprofit educational purposes;
- the nature of the copyrighted work;
- the amount and substantiality of the portion used in relation to the copyrighted work as a whole;
- the effect of the use upon the potential market for or value of the copyright work.

Educators should have little or no trouble complying with the "purpose and character of the work" factor. Teachers generally copy materials to aid the educational process. It should be noted, however, that recreational use of copied materials such as videocassettes, DVDs, CDs, or computer games is generally not allowed under the statute.

"The nature of the copyrighted work" factor can prove a bit more problematic than "character and purpose of the work." Who determines what is the nature of the work – the creator and/or copyright holder, the person making the copies, the judge and/or the jury? Almost any material can be classified as educational in some context; even a cartoon can be found to have some educational purpose if one is willing to look for it. It seems reasonable that, in determining "nature," a court would look to the ordinary use of the work and to the author's intent in creating the work.

The "amount and substantiality" of the work copied is especially troublesome in the use of videocassettes and computer programs. Teachers understand that they are not supposed to copy a whole book, but may not understand that copying a television program or a movie onto videotape or copying a computer program for student use can violate the "amount and substantiality" factor.

In the case of *Encyclopedia Britannica v. Crooks*, an educational company engaged in copying commercially available tapes and television programs for teachers, was found to be in violation of the Copyright Act. The company argued that it was providing an educational service for students and teachers who would otherwise be deprived of important educational opportunities. The court rejected the argument.

Educators may be tempted to think that their small-scale copying acts could not compare with the scope of the activities in this case. In the majority of instances involving single copying, there is no comparison. However the practice of teachers and, in some cases, of schools developing libraries of copies, is extremely problematic. Whether the collections are of print materials or non-print materials, the practice of building collections can easily be subjected to the same scrutiny as the *Encyclopedia* case.

The last of the four factors, "effect on the market," is also difficult to apply in the educational setting. Arguments can be advanced that students would not rent or purchase commercially available items, even if the copies weren't available. It appears, though, that use of an author's work without appropriate payment for the privilege, is a form of economic harm. Good faith generally will not operate as an acceptable defense in educational copyright or infringement cases.

Guidelines

A congressional committee developed *"Guidelines for Classroom Copying in Not-for-Profit Educational Institutions,"* printed in House Report 94-1476, 94th Congress 2d Sess.

(1976). Administrators should ensure that staff members have access to copies of the guidelines, which are readily available from local libraries, the Copyright Office, and members of Congress. Although these guidelines do not have the force of law that the statute has, judges have used them in deciding cases. Some examples of the guidelines follow.

For poetry, copying of a complete poem of less than 250 words printed on no more than two pages or of an excerpt of 250 words from a longer poem is allowed. For prose, a complete work of less than 2,500 words or an excerpt from a longer work of not more than 1,000 words or 10% of the work is permissible. The guidelines mandate that copying meet this test of *brevity*.

The copying must be *spontaneous*. The educator must have decided more or less on the spur of the moment to use an item. Spontaneity presumes that a person did not have time to secure permission for use from the copyright holder. A teacher or catechist who decides in September to use certain materials in December has ample time to seek permission. In such a situation, failure to seek permission means that the spontaneity requirement will not be met.

A last requirement is that the copying must not have a *cumulative effect*. Making copies of poems or songs by one author would have a cumulative effect and would mean that collected works of the author would not be bought. Similarly, as indicated above, the practice of "librarying" (building a collection of taped television programs, for example) is not permitted. Copying computer programs is never advisable, unless permission to make copies is included in the purchase or rental agreement.

Videos may be kept for 45 days only. During the first 10 days, a teacher or other educator may use the tape once in a class (although there is a provision for one repetition for legitimate instructional review). For the remaining 35 days educators may use the tape for evaluative purposes only.

Technology: Moral, Ethical & Legal Challenges

Twenty-five years ago – most educators and certainly most Catholic educators – had limited access to computer technology. Today it is hard to imagine life without computers and the related technology of the Information Age. Access to volumes of information that would have taken much time to gather a few years ago can now be obtained in a few moments with the aid of a modem and a database. These developments, wonderful as they are, present challenges for the educator who seeks to act in ways that are morally, ethically, and legally correct.

If a teacher is charged with copyright violation, it is likely that the principal will be charged as well. Clear policies and careful monitoring of those policies can lessen exposure to liability. As many legal authorities have observed, copyright violation is stealing. It appears, then, as a colleague of this author once stated, that *"Thou shalt not steal"* remains good law. At the very least, schools should adopt a policy requiring compliance with copyright laws.

Educators themselves must be models of integrity and observe the laws that grant authors and other creators the right to the fruits of their labors. Obviously, the Internet and the Information Highway were not part of Jesus' lived experience, but it is important to reflect on how He would want us to meet the challenges they present in today's world. Catholic educators must surely model their behavior on that of Jesus who scrupulously paid the temple tax, rendered Caesar his due, and exhorted landowners to pay workers a generous wage.

CHAPTER SEVEN

A FINAL REFLECTION:
IS IT LEGAL? IS IT ETHICAL?
CAN I DO IT? SHOULD I DO IT?

In this text, the author has attempted to outline the provisions of civil law as they affect Catholic schools and their communities. The text also offers suggestions that the author hopes may be helpful to administrators and teachers as they minister in the day-to-day lived reality of Catholic education. In this final chapter, the author hopes to offer some thoughts for reflection

After years of service in Catholic education, the author is firmly convinced that Catholic educators cannot simply ask: *"Can I legally do this?"* as a gauge for the rightness and wrongness of actions. Rather they must ask: *"Looking at what the law requires and the Gospel demands, what should I do? What would Jesus do?"* The latter are far more difficult questions than the first one and yet, as Catholic educators, we cannot simply consult legal texts for answers. Instead, all Catholic educators must search their hearts and consciences for the "right" answers and act accordingly.

The following quotation from T.S. Eliot's play, *Murder in the Cathedral*, has long intrigued the author: *"The last temptation is the greatest treason; to do the right deed for the wrong reason."* Not only must Catholic educators search for the "right" solutions to difficulties, they must search their motivations as well. For it is only when one is honest with oneself, that one can know the true peace of a decision well made.

Catholic educators daily face complex situations that may seem to call for the wisdom of Solomon, the tact of a public relations firm, and the faith of a saint. Many crises do not fit into "textbook solutions." Civil law may allow one action, but conscience may prescribe another path, one that is not simply legal but is also right. Just because the law allows a person to do something doesn't mean the person has to do it. Yes, the harried principal who has "had it" with the teacher who has made one too many mistakes, can simply say: *"I'm not choosing to renew your contract this year."* But the principal whose life is modeled on Christ must do more. He or she must search the heart and look at motivation. *"Am I doing this [not renewing the contract] because it is the best action to take for everyone or am I doing it because it is the easiest, most convenient action to take?"* Some questions need to be asked and answered. Has the teacher been given notice that performance is not acceptable? How long has the deficiency been apparent? Has the teacher been given any help or mentoring to improve? Is there some personal problem exacerbating the situation?

The noted columnist, Dolores Curran, once observed: *"Our church can be a lousy employer."* What is a sixty-year-old single female who has never taught anywhere else but in one school going to do if her contract is not renewed? The answer, of course, is not the legal responsibility of the principal. But, what about the moral responsibility? These questions should not be understood as suggesting that it is acceptable for teachers to be sub-standard in performance; rather, they suggest careful reflection and prayer for guidance before action.

Or consider the troublesome parent who has been a "thorn in the side" of school staff all year, who seems to be "at the bottom" of every complaint and dissatisfaction. It is tempting to refuse registration forms and fees for the next school year. After all, there is no contractual obligation to continue a child's enrollment from year to the other, is there? Yet, how will forcing that child to leave the school affect the child? What if the student is blameless and perhaps even embarrassed by parental behavior?

The student who technically merits expulsion poses a third example. Some years ago, the author was conducting a "beginning of the year" workshop for a high school faculty. Arriving early, she heard the principal explain to the faculty that he was "taking back" a student who had been dismissed the previous year. He stated that he believed the student had changed, had accepted responsibility for his misdeeds, and deserved a second chance. Some of the teachers were less than pleased. Should the principal have refused to allow the student a second chance? Certainly, he would have been within his rights to do so. The principal faced a tough decision. No doubt, he prayed about it. He knew he was risking faculty displeasure and the possibility that the student might "mess up" again. He chose to do what he thought was right, even though an easier, perfectly legal alternative existed. Similarly, a teacher can "throw" a disorderly student out of class or make the harder decision to work with that child.

After all, where would we be if Jesus gave up on us when we make mistakes? In the final analysis, we shall all be judged not merely on what we have chosen to do but on why we have chosen to do it.

These thoughts are not an attempt to suggest that there are no times when teachers or parents should be separated from the school. They do suggest, however, that decisions should not be made precipitously by one who is attempting to "teach as Jesus did." Jesus did not shield persons from the consequences of their actions, but He did show mercy, an important point to remember when one is tempted to give up on an individual or situation.

A Model for Legal/Ethical Decision Making

It is easy to identify legal principles and decide behavior on the basis of those principles. It is not so easy to decide what one ought to do. The question should not be: "Is this what I can legally do?" but rather: "Is this what I should do?" One way to reflect on issues and decisions is to use a legal/ethical decision-making model. Six steps are suggested.

(1) **Gather all relevant information.**

Things are not always as they first appear. Facts are

important, of course, but so are the reasons behind the facts. Is the problematic teacher's spouse out of work? Is the troublesome student facing the loss of a parent due to divorce or illness?

(2) **Identify legal issues.**

If you are not sure of the issues, ask for help from the diocesan office or the school attorney. Don't guess what the law might say. Get competent legal advice.

(3) **Identify moral/ethical issues.**

It is perfectly acceptable and not a sign of weakness to seek help in making this identification. Ask a peer what he or she sees as the issues. Or ask for a response on your own reading of the issues.

(4) **List and consider possible courses of action.**

Even if you are not sure that you would take a particular course of action, list it. Give yourself some time to consider the alternatives. Don't jump into action – if you can possibly wait.

(5) **Ask yourself, "What would Jesus do?"**

This is not a quick, academic exercise. Pray and ask for guidance.

(6) **Make your decision.**

A Final Word

It can be very tempting to worry about legal issues and forget the rest. All of us who minister in Catholic education must remember that we are all part of the family of God. Those of us who have responsibility for the lives of others should always ask: *"Is this the right thing to do? Are there less painful or difficult alternatives? How will I feel about this next year? In ten years? Is this the way I would want to be treated if I were in this situation? What would Jesus do?"* On the last day, we will be better served by having considered Jesus' viewpoint in addition to the requirements of civil law in our decision-making.

APPENDIX

ESTABLISHING BOUNDARIES BETWEEN CATHOLIC MEMORIAL EMPLOYEES/VOLUNTEERS AND STUDENTS
(used with permission)

As a school, Catholic Memorial wishes to encourage healthy relationships of mutual respect and trust between students, employees and volunteers. However, when dealing with students or recent graduates under the age of twenty-one, employees and volunteers must always conduct themselves in a manner that is above and beyond approach. Student safety is, and must be, paramount. When dealing with students and recent graduates under the age of twenty-one, employees and volunteers are required to conduct themselves in a manner that is always professional, avoiding all behavior and/or language that can violate the necessary, healthy distance that must be maintained at all times between adults and students.

As adults in positions of responsibility and authority, it is incumbent upon us to establish good boundaries with students. Good boundaries are the result of adult awareness and intro-spection. Good intentions are not enough to protect against the appearance of impropriety. As adults dealing with young people, we must ask ourselves not only, *"What do I intend?"* but *"How might my words and actions appear to someone else?"* When students address us with such titles as "Mr." or "Mrs." or "Brother' or "Coach" it should remind us that our relationships with students are *always* professional.

In light of this, the following policies must be strictly followed by Catholic Memorial employees and volunteers when dealing with Catholic Memorial students and recent Catholic Memorial graduates under the age of twenty-one.

Numbers 1 through 6 require specific approval by the President/Principal or their designee:

1. Off campus contact that is school-sponsored or school-sanctioned must always be treated as a school field trip. With the exception of normally scheduled athletic practices or competitions, all such activities require parental permission in writing (fax or e-mail is acceptable).

2. No Catholic Memorial student or recent graduate under the age of twenty-one is allowed into the home or vehicle of a Catholic Memorial employee or volunteer without the expressed permission of the student's parents or guardians.

3. Employees and volunteers may not socialize or meet off-campus with Catholic Memorial students or graduates under the age of twenty-one – unless the parent or guardian has given expressed permission for the meeting or is present.

4. Employees and volunteers are not permitted to provide professional services (i.e. tutoring, counseling, legal, physical condition/therapy) outside of the regular terms of employment to Catholic Memorial students or recent graduates under the age of twenty-one.

5. Employees and volunteers are not permitted to hire for any personal purpose, Catholic Memorial students or recent graduates under the age of twenty-one. Similarly, employees are not permitted to accept student "volunteers" for personal needs, services or projects.

6. Outside of regular school hours or regularly defined duties, employees and and volunteers are not to meet privately at Catholic Memorial with Catholic Memorial students or graduates under the age of twenty-one.

7. Electronic communication between students and employees/volunteers is only permitted through the Catholic Memorial e-mail system and/or websites hosted by Catholic Memorial.

8. When contacting a student at home, every attempt must be made to speak speak with the parent/guardian as well.

9. Employees and volunteers must never discuss with Catholic Memorial students or recent graduates under the age of twenty-one the problems, deficiencies or challenges of any school employee or Catholic Memorial student unless that person's well being is in question.

10. With regards to issues of confidentiality, employees and volunteers are to offer a disclaimer for Catholic Memorial student confidence: *"I can keep confidence only if it is about something not harmful to you or others."*

11. Employees and volunteers must not share intimate, personal and/or family information with Catholic Memorial students, In addition, employees and volunteers should not give personal phone numbers or personal e-mail addresses to Catholic Memorial students.

12. Employees and volunteers must not permit and/or join in any bullying of Catholic Memorial students. Employees are obliged to stop bullying and to admonish student(s) that such behavior is unacceptable.

13. Employees and volunteers should never tease students, adopt a deriding, sarcastic tone, or use racial, sexual, vulgar or provocative language. Such behavior has no place in our school and runs counter to our school values and philosophy.

14. Employees should never threaten students with secrecy such as, *"this must stay in the classroom/locker room,"* or *"I am only going to tell this to you but you can't tell your parents,"* etc.

Catholic Memorial takes seriously its moral and legal obligation to protect students from physical and sexual abuse. All allegations of employee or volunteer impropriety involving Catholic Memorial students or recent Catholic Memorial graduates under the age of twenty-one will be thoroughly investigated.

GLOSSARY OF TERMS

Board
A board (committee/council/commission) is a body whose members are selected or elected to participate in educational decision-making at the diocesan, regional, inter-parish or parish level.

Board with Limited Jurisdiction
A board with limited jurisdiction has power limited to certain areas of educational concern. It has final, but not total, jurisdiction in certain areas.

Collegiality
Collegiality is the sharing of responsibility and authority. In the Catholic Church, bishops have the highest authority within a diocese. Powers may be delegated to other parties, such as boards.

Common Law
Common law is that law not created by a legislature. It includes principles of action based on long-established standards of reasonable conduct and on court judgments affirming such standards. It is sometime called "judge-made law."

Compelling State Interest
Compelling state interest is the overwhelming or serious need for governmental action. The government is said to have a compelling state interest in anti-discrimination legislation and in the elimination of unequal treatment of citizens.

Consensus
As distinguished from majority rule, consensus is a model of decision-making in which a board seeks to arrive at a decision that all members can agree to support.

Consultative (advisory) Board
A consultative board is one which cooperates in the policy-making process by formulating and adapting, but never enacting, policy.

Contract

A contract is an agreement between two parties. The essentials of a contract are: (1) mutual assent (2) by legally competent parties (3) for consideration (4) to subject matter that is legal and (5) in a form of agreement that is legal.

Defamation

Defamation is an unprivileged communication. It can be either spoken (slander) or written (libel.)

Due Process (constitutional)

Due process is fundamental fairness under the law. There are two types:

Substantive Due Process: The constitutional guarantee that no person shall be arbitrarily deprived of his life, liberty, or property; the essence of substantive due process is protection from arbitrary unreasonable action (Black). Substantive due process concerns *what* is done as distinguished from *how* it is done (procedural due process).

Procedural Due Process: how the process of depriving someone of something is carried out; *how it is done*. The minimum requirements of Constitutional due process are *notice* and a *hearing* before an *impartial tribunal.*

Fiduciary

A fiduciary is one who has accepted the responsibility for the care of people or property.

Foreseeability

Foreseeability is the *"the reasonable anticipation that harm or injury is the likely result of acts or omission"* (Black). It is not necessary that a person anticipate the particular injury that might result from an action, but only that danger or harm in general might result.

Invasion of Privacy

Invasion of privacy is a tort action in which the plaintiff alleges that the defendant has unreasonably invaded personal privacy, e.g., revealing confidential information in student or personal files without the individual's consent.

Judicial Restraint
Judicial restraint is the doctrine that courts will not interfere in decisions made by professionals.

Landmark Court Decisions
Landmark court decisions are decisions of major importance. These decisions are often used as judicial reasoning in later decisions.

Negligence
Negligence is the absence of the degree of care which a reasonable person would be expected to use in a given situation. Legal negligence requires the presence of four elements: duty, violation of duty, proximate cause, and injury.

Policy
A policy is a guide for discretionary action. Policy states *what* is to be done, not *how* it is to be done.

Proximate Cause
Proximate cause is a contributing factor to an injury. The injury was the result of or reasonably foreseeable outcome of the action or inaction said to be the proximate cause.

State Action
State action is the presence of the government in an activity to such a degree that the activity may be considered to be that of the government.

Tenure
Tenure is an expectation of continuing employment.

Tort
A tort is a civil or private wrong as distinguished from a crime.

BIBLIOGRAPHY

Alexander, Kern (1980). *School law*. St. Paul: West.

Agostini v. Felton, 138 L.Ed.2d 391 (1997).

Aguilar v. Felton, 105 S.Ct. 3232 (1985).

Anthony v. Syracuse University, 231 N.Y.S. 435, 224 App. Div. 487 (1928).

Bischoff v. Brothers of the Sacred Heart, La. App. 416 So. 2d 348 (1982).

Benitez v. NYC B.O.E. 543, N.Y.2d 29 (1989).

Black, Henry Campbell. *Black's law dictionary* (5th ed.) St. Paul: West, 1979).

Bob Jones v. United States, 103 S.Ct. 2017 (1983).

Brooks v. Logan and Joint District No. 2 903 P.2d 73 (1995).

Buckley Amendment of 1975.

CACE/NABE Governance Task Force (1987). *A Primer on Educational Governance in the Catholic Church*. Washington, D.C.: NCEA.

Civil Rights Act of 1964.

Copyright Act of 1976.

Curay-Cramer v. The Ursuline Academy of Wilmington, Delaware, Inc., et al., C.A. No. 03-1014-KAJ (November 16, 2004)

Davis v. Homestead Farms, 359 N.W.2d 1.

Encyclopedia Brittanica v. Crooks, 542 F. Supp. 1156 (W.D.N.Y. 1982).

Flint v. St. Augustine School High School

Geraci v. St. Xavier High School, 12 Ohio Op. 3d 146 (Ohio, 1978).

Gorman v. St. Raphael Academy, Sup. Ct. (R.I.) No. 2003-371-Appeal (PC01-4821, July 15, 2004.)

Gott v. Berea College, 156 Ky. 376 (1913).

"Guidelines for Classroom Copying in Not-for-Profit Educational Institutes," *House Report* 94-1476, 94th Congress 2d Session (1976).

"Guidelines for Off-Air Recording of Broadcast Programming for Educational Purposes," CONG. REC.E4750 (daily edition October 14, 1981).

Individuals with Disabilities in Education Act (1997).

Keiser v. Catholic Diocese of Shreveport, Inc., Ct. of Appeals, 2d Circ., No. 38, 797 CA (Louisiana, 2004).

Levandowski v. Jackson City School Distrcit, 328 S.2d 339 (Minn. 1976).

Little v. St. Mary Magdalene, 739 F.Supp. 1003 (1990).

Marcus v. Rowley, 695 F.2d 1171 (1983).

New Jersey v. T.L.O., 105 S. Ct. 733 (1985).

NLRB v. Catholic Bishop of Chicago, 440 U.S. 490 (1979).

Pastoral Statement of U.S. Catholic Bishops on Handicapped People (1978).

Peterman v. International Brotherhood of Teamsters Local 396, 174 Cal.App.2d 184, 344 P.2d 25 (1959).

Pierce v. the Society of Sisters, 268 U.S. 510 (1925).

Public Law 94-142, Education of All Handicapped Children Act.

Reardon v. LeMoyne et al., 454 A.2d 428 (N.H. 1982).

Rendell-Baker v. Kohn, 102 S.Ct. 2764 (1982).

Reutter, E.E., Jr. (1981). *Schools and the law.* Reston, Virginia: National Association of Secondary School Principals.

Robert, Henry M. III et al., *Robert's Rules of Order* (10th ed). Cambridge, MA: Perseus, 2000.

Section 504 of the Rehabilatation Act of 1973 (amended 1974).

Smith v. Archbishop of St. Louis, 632 S.W.2d 516 (1982).

Stetson University v. Hunt, 88 Fla. 510 (1924).

Tinker v. Des Moines Independent Community School District et al., 393 U.S. 503 (1969).

Titus v. Lindberg, 228 A.2d 65 (N.J., 1967).

United States Code Annotated.

United States Constitution.

Weithoff v. St. Veronica's School, 210 N.W.2d 108 (Mich. 1973).

Wisch v. Sanford School, Inc., 420 F. Supp. 1310 (1976).

Wood v. Strickland, 420 U.S. 308 (1975).

www.StopHazing.org